J. C. Buttre Sc.

Sarah D. Comstock

MEMOIR

OF

MRS. SARAH D. COMSTOCK,

Missionary to Arracan.

BY MRS. A. M. EDMOND.

In the desert let me labor,
On the mountain let me tell
How he died,—the blessed Saviour,
To redeem a world from hell.
Let me hasten
Far in heathen lands to dwell.

S. F. SMITH.

Philadelphia:
AMERICAN BAPTIST PUBLICATION SOCIETY,
118 ARCH STREET.

Contents.

CHAPTER V.

CHAPTER VI.

CHAPTER VII,

CHAPTER VIII.

CHAPTER IX.

CHAPTER X.

CHAPTER XI.

CHAPTER XII.

MEMOIR.

CHAPTER I.

Her Early Years—Consecration to God—Devotion—Sabbath School Class.

She came to the Saviour in life's happy morning;
And gave her young heart to its Maker's control,
When the rose in its freshness her cheek was adorning,
And the glad eye was beaming the hopes of the soul.
With a spirit all glowing with grateful emotion,
His mercies she tasted, his truths she adored,
And sought with sincere and unwearied devotion,
Henceforth to do only the will of her Lord.

THE motives which stimulate to action the true Missionary are the purest and most sublime that can animate the human soul. They are Divine in their origin, being emanations of the same spirit of heavenly love which brought the Redeemer of mankind to the performance of his labors upon earth, and to that wonderful death on the Cross, which secures everlasting life and joy to an innumerable number of the human race.

The warrior as he goes to battle is inspired by hope, the hope of martial glory, which urges him boldly on to the reward of patriotism and valor; the scholar perseveringly toils through the weary day, and even until the midnight hours are spent, to accomplish those mental achievements which shall win for him the bright laurels of fame. Self-aggrandizement stimulates the majority of mankind in the great struggles of life.

But the Missionary who sacrifices his dearest earthly interests, and isolates himself from sacred privileges and congenial society, to journey into strange lands, and take up his abode amidst scenes of idolatry, vice, and sufferings, giving the vigor of his life to the work of evangelization, is inspired by no shining visions of earthly recompense. His actions are the offspring of a genuine benevolence. Love and compassion for the souls of his fellow men, and the desire of glorifying God, enable him to endure patiently, even joyfully the hardships of an existence which possesses no charms but these.

Disinterested benevolence is one of the grand features of Christianity. He who feels the love of God shed abroad in his heart, who sees the worth of the soul, and the preciousness of the salvation that redeems it, becomes desirous that others should experience like emotions, and be sharers in the same hopes and bliss. Hence arises the resolution of self-devotion to labors for this end. It springs not from the impulse of a moment, but from the prayerful, humble, thoughtful consideration of days, months, and often years. Once formed, and viewed as the fruit of Divine influence, it is adhered to with unflinching firmness. Whole-souled consecration to God and firmness of purpose go hand in hand, and constitute two leading elements in the character of a Missionary.

These qualities were beautifully and strikingly combined in the character of the beloved one, who is the subject of this Memoir; recollections of whose life we would gather up as precious memorials, dear both to religion and friendship.

Let us draw gently aside the veil of time from the past, and review the Christian career of this devoted and useful laborer in the vineyard of the Lord.

Sarah Davis, afterward Mrs. Comstock, was born in Brookline, Massachusetts, September 24th, 1812.

She possessed naturally an uncommonly lively temperament, great warmth of affection, and much resolution.

Her father died when she was of an early age, and her youthful days passed away under the careful training of a pious and efficient mother, whose own energetic spirit found a more striking development in that of her child.

She was uniformly obedient to her parents, and kind to her associates, finding the perfection of her own happiness in the enjoyment of those around her, to which she contributed with hearty good will. She was always very frank in the expression of her opinions and feelings, while at the same time she took great care not to injure those of others. A union of sincerity with courteousness formed a very pleasant trait in her character.

Possessing by nature a keen perception

and relish for enjoyment, the season of childhood and youth was to her a period of unusual delight; yet, when in her sixteenth year she stood on the verge of womanhood, and gazed into the vista opening before her, she found even in her full happy heart, a void, where a deeper, holier joy was wanting than earth could ever bestow.

She felt too the claims of her Creator upon her *supreme* love and obedience. Though so amiable in her deportment and full of tender regard for her friends, she became convinced that she had deeply sinned in having so long withheld her best affections from God; and was conscious of possessing no power of herself to atone for this deficiency. She saw clearly also, that the human heart can never meet the requirements of the law, so broad and searching in its demands. By the influences of the Holy Spirit she was thus taught her need of a Saviour, whom she sought sorrowing, until the sweet peace of his presence brought an assurance of pardon to her soul, and acceptance with God through his atoning sacrifice. She gave her young heart to him freely and unreservedly; and, overflowing with love and gratitude to one who had done so much for her, became immediately and intensely solicitous that others should experience the same precious hopes and joys.

And now we see plainly and almost unceasingly manifested in the early part of her Christian career, the same deep interest, and heartfelt anxiety for the cause of the unconverted among the circles of her home influence—the germs of that devoted spirit, which she afterwards manifested and developed in a more extended sphere, when she entered an ardent laborer into the fields of Missionary enterprise.

It seemed her delight to converse upon religious subjects with all who were willing to listen. Her heart longed to attract others to the same Saviour who had become so precious to her own soul. These desires increased with her advancement in religious experience, and for this end her prayers and labors became frequent and warm. The fruits of a genuine conversion are mainly, a spirit of frequent and fervent prayer, love and study of the Bible close self-examination, ardent faith in God, and a strong determination to know and do his will. All these became apparent in the unfolding of Mrs. Comstock's Christian character.

Soon after her conversion she felt it to be her desire, as well as high privilege, to connect herself with the people of God.

Her scriptural views of the ordinance of baptism were so clear and convincing, she felt it her duty to unite with a church of the Baptist denomination. Accordingly she presented herself before the Baptist Church in her native town and related her Christian experience, which was listened to with much interest and pleasure; and on the 4th of April, 1830, she made a public profession of her faith by baptism, and was received as a member of the church.

About this time she was engaged in teaching a day school for children. So deep an interest did she take in their spiritual condition, that she frequently imparted to them religious instruction, prayed with them, and entreated them to come to the Saviour, who has said, "Suffer little children to come

2

unto me and forbid them not, for of such is the kingdom of heaven."

Some of the parents, whose sentiments differed from her own, were averse to her religious influence and removed their children to another school. But the good seed sown was not lost. Mrs. Comstock relates, in a letter to an absent sister, that these little ones sought opportunities of meeting her, desirous of hearing from her lips the sweet words of eternal life, and of having her engage with them in prayer as she had been accustomed to do.

To her class in the Sabbath school she was warmly attached. She *longed* for their conversion to God; to her their souls were unspeakably dear. With tears and prayers and earnest entreaties, she sought to awaken in their youthful hearts a saving interest in Divine things. Her efforts in their behalf were unwearied, and her prayers almost unceasing. Even the midnight hour bore witness to her earnest supplication at a Throne of Grace. On one occasion a friend, who passed the night at her father's house, was awakened from sleep by sounds which he perceived to be the earnest tones of a human voice; he arose and listened; in an adjoining chamber, he recognized the voice of Mrs. Comstock in fervent entreaties that God would have mercy upon her beloved class. Her spirit seemed to agonize in prayer for their salvation. It appeared as if like Jacob, when he wrestled with the angel, she could not cease her importunities except she received assurance of a blessing.

In the providence of God, a revival of religion occurred in B——, and extended to some of the members of the Sabbath school who became the children of hope and grace. Two of Mrs. Comstock's class were among the number. This event occasioned in their teacher the most intense feeling and rejoicing, and redoubled her anxiety in behalf of the others.

In a letter to an absent sister written at this time, adverting to the religious prospects of the community, she expresses her her deep emotions upon this subject.

"You know, my dear sister," she remarks, "how deeply I have felt interested in the cause of Sabbath schools, particularly in our own, and *especially in my own class*, the salvation of whose precious souls has long occupied a prominent place in my heartfelt desires. As an instrument in the hands of God, I have labored for their conversion; my most earnest entreaties at the Throne of Grace have been offered in their behalf, and the most generous offerings of thought and affection have been sacrificed at the altar of their *spiritual interests*. You know not, nor can I describe to you, what have at times been my feelings for these dear ones. O the thought that those who possess so many amiable and endearing qualities, and traits of character, should be content without possessing the one thing needful is exquisitely painful. I have sometimes thought my feelings in some faint degree might resemble those of the Saviour, when the interesting inquiry, 'What shall I do to inherit eternal life?' was addressed to him, by a youth, whose moral character was *equally interesting*.

As I behold, I cannot but love them; but I sometimes feel *constrained* almost, to take them by the hand and lead them to Christ. I cannot endure the thought that they are living in rejection of the kind invitations and entreaties of the Saviour—the precious Saviour who has done so much for them.

With feelings such as these, you would suppose I should witness with no common sensations the ordinance of baptism administered to the first of these dear ones who gave evidence of having become a child of God. The season I spent in the Sabbath school that morning was unusually interesting. I endeavored to make the remainder of the class *feel* that A—— was about to give them the parting hand. The whole class were affected, even to tears, and indeed my feelings would not suffer *me* to proceed. O it was a melting—a precious season—nor less so was last Sabbath. The feelings manifested on the preceding were I think increased, and what was still more delightful, during the past week, L——, another of my class had entertained a hope of having passed from death to life. I would tell you—but—I cannot—language is inadequate to express the gratitude I felt when I heard of this instance of the goodness of the Lord. L—— has long been a subject of anxious solicitude.

I have watched with an eye of deep interest the first dawn, and the progress of conviction on her mind. I have carried her daily, and at times, I might almost say, hourly, in the arms of earnest supplication to the Mercy Seat—and O! when I saw so gracious an answer to my prayers, although I had long anticipated this event, I could not believe the evidence of my senses. O! how miserably deficient are we in faith, oftentimes, my dear sister! We pray for needed and greatly desired blessings, and that perhaps with long perseverance, yet when we actually receive those blessings, we manifest almost as little interest as though we never asked for them.

The case of L—— is one of peculiar interest if we consider her situation as a poor little orphan, destitute, I might almost say, of friends, at least, of near relatives; yet I trust the promise, 'when thy father and thy mother forsake thee, then the Lord will take thee up,' has been fulfilled in her case. You would be delighted to see and converse with her; her heart is full to overflowing with love to her Saviour, and she wishes to urge upon all her young companions, the importance of accepting him *now* in their youthful days. I hope the impressions and feelings which this circumstance has imparted, will not soon be effaced from my mind, and while it serves as an encouragement for continued exertion, it has, I trust, made me feel more sensibly my dependence upon Almighty power for success in whatever undertaking I engage. *I know* that every effort I *have made* or *can make is vain unless* sanctified by Divine Grace; therefore, give God the glory, for the work is his alone. He is indeed a wonder-working God, and, my dear sister, let us in future repose unshaken confidence in Him, as *our God*, and the supplier of all our wants. How happy should we be, oftentimes, compared with what we are, did we but believe the express declarations of that Being who cannot lie, and whose purposes change not, or, in other words, did we pursue such a course of conduct as is consonant with such a belief.

But to return to my subject from which I have widely digressed, I will add that others of my dear class are serious. You cannot con ceive what pleasure is imparted by the fond anticipation of seeing *all* of them ere long, *sincere followers of the Redeemer.* Could anything be more delightful than to see a juvenile band like this traveling hand in hand toward the 'Mount of God.'"

The efforts of this faithful teacher were not unrewarded. Her whole class, nine in number, were ultimately hopefully converted. Though some lingered on the threshold of the Ark of Safety, until their beloved friend had gone to labor for the souls of the perishing heathen, not one seal at last was wanting to her full success, and in after years they remembered with affectionate gratitude, her, who had been the instrument in Divine Providence of directing their feet to the way of life.

CHAPTER II.

Religious Exercises—Letters to a Sister—Impulses toward Missionary labor—Convictions of duty—Letter to her Parents—Decision.

> **From shores beyond the swelling sea,**
> **Where mighty Error holds its sway—**
> **There comes the heathen's earnest plea,**
> **For tidings of salvation's way.**
> **Who from these ranks of ours shall go,**
> **A guide to brighter worlds on high?**
> **Wouldst thou, thy duty, Christian, know?**
> **Lift up thy voice,—Lord, is it I?**

Mrs. Comstock attached great importance to the cultivation of *vital piety,* as necessary to the life and growth of a Christian.

In her estimation, no pursuits, however, attractive should be followed to the detriment of the superior claims of religion. Her chief aim was to progress in spiritual graces. As an aid to such advancement, she considered rigid and frequent *self-examination* a most important and indispensable duty, with which no other should interfere.

But her views on these subjects are best learned from her own language used in letters written to her sister. She commences with venturing a word of caution against indulging too ardent an interest in literary pursuits, lest it engender a neglect of the cultivation of vital piety, and remarks thus,

"I know from experience, my dear L——, that there is a propensity in the human heart to substitute innumerable excuses, (of which the *indispensableness of such attainments* is not the least palpable,) for the superficial performance of devotional duties. But I cannot endure the thought, of a decline in *your* religious affections, and I cannot but repeat to you the warning addressed to *me* a few days since by an an aged saint, who is now on the confines of the eternal world. Standing by the bedside of the dying sufferer, and witnessing her almost insupportable agony, I said, 'I hope you will soon be beyond the reach of suffering, for your pilgrimage has nearly ended.' With an expression almost unearthly she fixed her eye upon me, and replied with unusual emphasis, 'I hope so, but, my dear S——, *you* have just commenced *your* journey; the road is full of danger, and you will meet with many trials—many temptations—and you cannot of yourself overcome them; but you must watch and pray. *O be constantly watchful and prayerful* that you enter not into temptation.'

"This, dear L——, is salutary advice, did we but follow it. What duties *can* be more important to the Christian, yet how often do we greatly, and at times, *almost* entirely neglect them, and how much keen remorse should we spare ourselves were we more faithful in this respect.

"Another duty nearly allied to these is *self-examination:* this is indispensably necessary to an assurance of a well-grounded hope of an interest in Christ. A merely superficial inspection once a month or once a week is not sufficient. The merchant who neglects his accounts day after day, and week after week, finds his affairs strangely deranged; and they cannot be regulated without spending much time in perplexing reviews, when at the same time, all confusion might easily have been avoided, and order and regularity preserved by the daily bestowal of a few moments attention.

"And so, my dear sister, if we would have our souls to prosper we must daily bring them to the touchstone of Divine truth, and *faithfully* try them by that unerring standard. In seasons of spiritual declension, we are too apt to suffer our souls to be lulled to sleep, if I may be allowed the expression, upon the pillow of past experience; but if we have not *present* evidence of piety, we have, I think, no *good reason* to hope, that we are in a regenerate state. By this, I would not insinuate, that a high degree of enjoyment at all times is essential to such evidence; far from it; too much dependence is oftentimes placed, by *young Christians especially*, upon particular frames of mind. An even and constantly moderate degree of religious happiness is far more desirable, in my opinion, than temporary, and *merely temporary* excitement; for seasons of depression equal to the excitement are sure to succeed such unwonted emotion.

"It is strictly true, I think, that 'religious

despondency is the natural offspring of religious enthusiam.'

"One who is a Christian cannot but acknowledge the correctness of this; how superior is the light that burns steadily, though not dazzlingly, to that which now flashes powerfully upon the surrounding darkness, and now is nearly extinguished by the passing wind. True, in the inequality and excitability of our natures, we are subject to unusual emotions arising from unusual circumstances, yet He who is our great Example, the same yesterday, to-day and forever, desires His followers to be spiritually uniform in their faith and lives, never retrograding but ever striving and increasing. He who looks back to seasons of religious revival alone for testimonials of his Christian experience and, forward to their recurrence as necessary to a renewal of this, should beware lest the Lord of the vineyard come in an hour when it is barren and fruitless and take away his inheritance forever. It is upon what we *are*, not upon what we have been, that our religious estimate should be founded."

On another occasion, Mrs. Comstock remarks,

"O my dear sister, let me entreat you to stand fast in the Lord, and by a life of habitual piety, cheerful obedience, incessant prayer; and lively faith, prove that you are indeed a child of God, a vessel fit for the Master's use. Let no consideration for a single moment tempt you to neglect secret prayer, this is the life of the soul, the chief pillar in the building of faith; unsupported by this the edifice falls."

This is excellent advice from one young Christian to another; advice which all who love our Lord Jesus Christ, and are desirous of enjoying religion and growing in grace, would do well to heed. Secret prayer is most powerful to preserve our wandering hearts; it is the Christian's armor, which should be kept unceasingly bright, and never laid aside. Without it we become defenceless indeed; the world creeps in; its errors blind our souls; its vanities excite our desires, and in eagerly pursuing them, we lose sight of those superior attractions which are the gifts of our Lord himself, and which he bestows upon the earnest supplicant at the Throne of Grace.

He who seeks to maintain a Christian course and neglects secret prayer, is like one who sails along a wild and stormy coast with no pilot to guide him from the hidden dangers, which, sooner or later, make shipwreck of the bark in whose strength he trusted, and which destroys his hopes forever.

At morn, at noon, and even, and at all needed times, let the true Christian lift his heart to God in prayer. So shall he live by the life of his Lord, the vine into which he is grafted; and like the abundant manna that descended in olden days, heavenly gifts shall fall upon his soul, strength, wisdom, and joy unspeakable and full of glory.

As Mrs. Comstock strove thus to grow in grace, so she increased in religious effort. Soon, her large and loving heart, so full of pious emotions, did not rest satisfied with its endeavors for the spiritual good alone of the friends she cherished and the dear Sabbath school class. Her overflowing sympathy, her ardent love for souls, often carried her thoughts beyond the sphere in which she was born, and had thus far labored, to distant regions of idolatry and darkness. To her, those for whose salvation she had been striving with prayers and tears, were like a few blades of wheat on the borders of a mighty field, which had greater need of a laborer's hand.

The vision of a heathen world perishing in ignorance and sin, touched the tenderest chords in her newly-sanctified nature, and like a dark but powerful picture, drew to itself her spiritual vision, until it absorbed her gaze.

The still small voice of the Holy Spirit whispered the Saviour's command, "Go, teach all nations," in the ear that had already caught the Macedonian cry, "Come over and help us;" and the desire grew more ardent, the resolve more strong, to depart and bear the glad tidings of salvation to distant regions. She was animated by no momentary fit of enthusiasm, no longing for fame, but, by a calm and deliberate conviction of *duty*, a deep sense of gratitude to the Saviour who had laid down his life for her salvation, and a love for souls, second only to her love for God.

Impressed as she powerfully was with feelings like these, we are not surprised that she wrote the following letter to her beloved parents, as soon as an opportunity seemed to present itself, by which she could carry out the desire of her heart. The letter will sufficiently explain itself without any farther introductory remark:—

Brookline, Dec. 25, 1832.

"MY DEAR PARENTS,

"You have seen the communications I received from Mr. Comstock, and must feel that the subject on which they treat is one of great importance. and merits a careful and deliberate consideration. I wish to act in such a way as shall secure the approbation of God. I wish to know all that my heavenly Father would have me to do; feeling at the same time a firm determination—firm beyond repentance—that every tie shall be severed, every trial surmounted, every sacrifice *cheerfully* made, that may come in contact with *my duty*. I know that this will inevitably subject me to many a painful and severe struggle with natural feelings; but in my covenant engagement I vowed to be the Lord's. Yes, 'I have opened my mouth, and I cannot,' I WISH NOT, to 'go back.' The pledge of entire consecration of all that I have and am, MUST be redeemed. Besides, while in the performance of duty—*stern duty*, have I not, my dear parents, everything to hope, and nothing to fear, from the mercy of a benevolent God? O! I cannot describe, for language fails to express the pleasure and comfort I have drawn from this passage of Divine inspiration—'Commit thy way unto the Lord, and he shall direct thy steps.' I would not, at this trying moment, part with this and similar expressions of paternal kindness for the wealth of Golconda.

"But to come more directly to the subject I wish to introduce for your consideration. I have long, as you are aware, contemplated the 'Missionary Enterprise' with intense interest. I *have* thought it might be my duty at some future time to engage personally in the glorious cause of man's salvation in heathen lands. I *now* feel that the time is come for me to decide whether Christ or my friends predominate in my affections When I think of a separation, a final separation, for this world, from my dear parents, beloved brothers, an affectionate sister, and other endeared friends;—religious privileges too,—nature is disposed to say, It is too much to think of—too great a sacrifice. But can I do *too much* to express my love to that precious Saviour, *who withheld not his own life for me?* Ah, no! my parents will concur with me in saying *I cannot.* Now I wish to ask *your full and free consent, to the only proof I have in my power to give, of my attachment to Christ*—that of devoting my life, a *sacrifice,* if he require it, to his cause in foreign lands. I ask, that you will consider this subject prayerfully, and decide in view of the retributions of 'the great day.' Upon your decision, and ultimately upon that of the Church and the 'Board,' rests my future course; for I cannot come to any decision that shall be counter to your wishes.

"Perhaps you will say, 'there is in your own country ample field for Missionary effort.' True! I *have,* and *do still* maintain that a Christian need not *want* opportunities for the exercise of benevolent feelings, wherever he may be. But many things are to be taken into consideration. Some places are more destitute than others; some situations require the exercise of greater self-denial—the endurance of more severe hardships than others. Many who are disposed to labor in the one, may be unable or unwilling to engage in the other. And as the number is small of those who are disposed to bid adieu to friends, home, etc., for the cause of their Redeemer, is it not the imperative duty of the few whom God has endued with this disposition, to cherish and exercise it? I know that I am entirely unworthy the great honor of being a co-worker with God,—unworthy the privilege of laboring for souls, and destitute of necessary piety and other qualifications, moral and intellectual; but to the source of every perfection I look for supplies of every deficiency. I know that my Heavenly Father will require the performance of no duty for which he will not impart needful grace.

"All that I have now to do is to submit

to you the result of much prayerful reflection,—that God calls me to his service in foreign lands, and request your approbation, as soon as you can give it. You will perceive that it is necessary for me to write to Mr. C. without delay, as he must necessarily be in a state of painful suspense until he knows my decision.

"I wish that nothing should be said or hinted to any one who is not now acquainted with the circumstances of my situation. Should your reply be such as I believe you will be constrained to give, I purpose soon to communicate my feelings to the church, for their consideration;—my feelings, I mean, in relation to the mission.

"Yours, affectionately,

"S. DAVIS."

Not long after her intentions of becoming a Missionary were made public, she remarks on this subject in writing to a friend:

"I have not, my dear S——, in coming to this important decision, been guided by that enthusiasm with which some may be ready to charge me; nor have I acted with that precipitancy which may perhaps justly be considered an ingredient in my character. No; my conduct is the result of calm, deliberate, and rational *reflection;* nor was it without many a struggle between conviction of duty and natural affection, many an agonizing prayer for Divine aid, that I could say, 'Thy will be done.'

"Never is the mystery of my being led to this undertaking more insoluble than when I consider my *unfitness* for so holy and responsible a station as that of a Missionary of the cross. And yet, I know *that* is nought to me, since thus God hath directed it; for what am I, that I should thus plead my weakness, and so limit the Almighty in whom all fullness dwells, to a certain degree of human power?

"I have no excuse that I *dare* offer for refusing to go to benighted Burmah. *I believe God has directed me thither*, and should I dissent, I know I could not, with unstained raiment, meet the heathen at the judgment bar; no, the wailings of those who perish without having heard of a Saviour's love, would upbraid me for my selfishness.

'Love of ease,
And all the cultured joys, conveniences,
And delicate delights of ripe society.'

"What though trials, suffering, and danger be my earthly lot, shall I fear to follow where my Saviour leads? Shall I shrink from persecution and reproach, or tremble before the stake, if the cause of Him, who withheld not *his life* for me, required this at my hands?

"Gratitude forbids it. Yes, and it seems even a privilege to be cast into the furnace for the sake of walking with Jesus. Though of myself I can do nothing, my strength being perfect weakness, yet I can do all things, and bear all sufferings if my Lord be there.

"Though unworthy the *high honor,* yet I I feel it will be my *privilege* to wear out life in winning souls to God."

Such was the heartfelt language of Mrs. Comstock upon this important subject. Who can listen to these truthful outpourings of her devoted spirit, and think that *her* consecration to the Missionary service was from other than the highest, purest motives, and her call aught but a call from on high.

CHAPTER III.

Preparation for the Work—Foretastes of Missionary Life—Views of Herself—Anticipations of the Future—Public Consecration—Embarkation—Parting Scenes.

Gladly she left her father's house,
  To toil in stranger lands;
To raise the Christian banner high,
  O'er Asia's burning sands;
O'er the dark multitudes who bend
  To senseless gods the knee;
Who know not Jesus bled and died
  Their captive souls to free.

Sweet home and friends she dearly loved,
  But more than these, the soul;
The ever-living soul of man,
  Enslaved by sin's control;
And deem'd no sacrifice too great
  Could she but one restore
From error's bonds to freedom's bliss
  And life forevermore.

IN the year 1832, Mrs. Comstock commenced carrying into action her long-cherished resolve of becoming a Missionary. She had conversed upon the subject at various intervals with her parents, her pastor, the Rev. Joseph A. Warne, to whom she was warmly attached, and with many others of her friends. None who listened to her could do otherwise than approve of her determination, so characterized was it by the spirit of true Christian devotion and sincerity of purpose.

She also related to the church in Brookline, with which she was connected, her exercises of mind with reference to devoting herself to missionary labor. The church listened with much interest to her deeply affecting recital, and afterwards passed the following resolutions:

"Whereas, our beloved sister, Sarah Davis, has related to us the exercises of her mind on the important and interesting subject of becoming a Missionary to the heathen; and, whereas, from this relation we are led to believe, that the Lord designs for her the honor of laboring in the Missionary field, and for us the honor of sacrificing to the Missionary cause our pleasure in her society, and our advantage in her labors among us, particularly in the Sabbath School, therefore,

"Resolved, That we are deeply interested in the recital to which we have listened of the special exercise of our beloved sister with relation to her becoming a laborer in the Missionary field; and, judging in the fear of God, it is our opinion, that, should the Board of Missions judge her qualified for the Missionary work, and be willing to receive her under their patronage, such coincidence of her desires for the work, with their willingness to employ her in it, will amount to a call to engage therein.

"Resolved, also, That judging the exercises she has related to have originated in pure desires for the glory of God, in the salvation of the perishing, and in the operation of the Divine Spirit on her heart; we dare not refuse our consent and even approbation of her purpose, though we most deeply feel the value of the sacrifice we are called to make of her labors in our various female meetings, and societies, and especially in the Sabbath school; labors, the lack of which we shall sensibly feel; yet we desire to say, 'the Lord gave and the Lord hath taken away.'

"Resolved, moreover, That this Church

hereby express to the relations of our dear sister, several of whom are members of our body, their sympathies and congratulations on this deeply interesting occasion, their sympathies in the affecting and in some sense irreparable loss they are likely to be called to sustain in the departure of our sister to a heathen land, and their congratulations that the Great Head of the Church has indulged them with the means of making to His cause among the heathen so precious an offering; and may they find His promise verified, that they who leave or forego children and sisters for His sake, and the Gospel's, shall be repaid 'a hundred fold in this life, and in the life everlasting.'

"Resolved, finally, That this Church furnish to our beloved sister from the hand of our pastor, a letter to the Secretary of the Board of Foreign Missions, certifying our cordial approbation of the step she is about to take, and our earnest recommendation of her to their patronage."

Afterwards she presented herself before the Board of Missions, held in Boston, as a candidate for Missionary service. About the same time, also, Rev. Grover S. Comstock, to whom she was afterwards united by marriage, offered himself for the same holy cause. Both were accepted, and appointed as laborers for the Mission in Burmah.

It was Mrs. Comstock's original intention to have gone forth alone as a Missionary, and to have resided in the family of some one of those who had preceded her; but a gracious Providence saw fit to order her lot otherwise in thus appointing to her a beloved companion and fellow-laborer. They were not married however until June 24, 1834, a few weeks before they sailed.

After her acceptance by the board, she spent nearly a year at Hamilton, New York, acquiring a knowledge of the Burman language, for which an excellent and unusual opportunity was afforded. Rev. Mr. Wade and his wife, returned Missionaries, accompanied by two native converts were then residing temporarily in that place.

From these friends she also gained much information respecting the land which was to be her future home. She heard of the trials and discouragements of Missionary life, of the sacrifices that must be made, and the obstacles that must be overcome; but she heard also, like a strain of glad music amid echoes of sadness, what great and exceeding joy is theirs who labor for God, and how precious, how glorious in the regions of sin and darkness, are the tidings of salvation and the light of Divine Truth.

In the humble but sincere converts brought from that far off Pagan land, she saw trophies of the grace that redeems, the religion that exalts mankind. Thousands and tens of thousands of souls, as precious as these, waited for the coming of a teacher who could guide their feet also into the paths of eternal life.

No prospect of probable peril or trial appalled her. She knew that hours, and perhaps days and weeks, of toil and suffering must inevitably attend her thither; but she swerved not from her determination, neither turned aside for a moment from the path which she had chosen.

Nor did the persuasions of beloved friends, or the keen sorrow, the agony that was gathering around her heart at the prospect of soon parting with them forever, affect for a moment her holy purpose.

Her heart only beat faster with courageous devotion as she consecrated herself anew to God's own enterprise, and she felt no emotions of regret save for what she considered her own unworthiness to assume its solemn responsibilities.

During Mrs. Comstock's stay in Hamilton, she seemed desirous of occupying all her spare moments for the benefit of those by whom she was surrounded; to become as it were, a Missionary at home, and to receive in some slight degree, though as far as possible, a foretaste of what she was hereafter to experience. Besides laboring for the spiritual benefit of those in the higher walks of life, she loved to seek out the abodes of the poor and wretched, and minister to their wants.

But Mrs. Comstock's labors of love while at Hamilton centered chiefly as they had done in Brookline, on the interests of the Sabbath school. The first Sabbath after her arrival she visited the school, and manifested a deep interest in its welfare.

The following account of her efforts there was originally furnished for one of our periodicals, in an article entitled "The Successful Teacher," by one who was then superintendent of the Baptist Sabbath School in Hamilton.

"She entered the school with a heart full of love and thirsting for usefulness. Soon she became acquainted with the teachers and superintendent, and in a few weeks, one of the teachers having left the school, the class was committed to her care. This class consisted of seven; she labored in connection with the school only about nine months; but she labored faithfully, and with success. During this time six of her class were converted, and united with the Baptist Church in that place; making thirteen, including those who were converted in her class in Brookline, who became pious in the Sabbath school through her immediate efforts in the short space of four years.

"But do any inquire, what was the secret of her success? We answer first, it may be found in her deep piety, manifesting itself in her immediate and all-absorbing object, the conversion of each individual of her class to God. This with her, was the primary thing, and what she desired and expected immediately to witness. She knew that every week the word of eternal truth would be to them a 'savor of life unto life, or of death unto death,' and with her, it was not a matter of indifference which.

"In the personal application of all her instructions to each one of her class, it was not sufficient that she talked to them in a general manner, but she was in the habit of conversing with each separately; of laying open to their view the nature and ruinous tendency of sin, and of appealing directly and pointedly to the conscience of each.

"In her manner of imparting instruction, there was nothing like indifference or coldness in her appearance; but her whole countenance, every feature, every expression, showed that she believed and felt what she said. In her eye, in the tones and inflections of her voice, and indeed in her whole appearance, her love for their souls was manifest, and her appeals and entreaties produced effect, as such appeals and entreaties always will. Hers was eloquence which art cannot produce. It was the powerful, the irresistible eloquence of a full and overflowing heart.

"She went from ardent prayer in her closet to her class, and carried with her the spirit of heaven, which she there imbibed in communion with her God. She remembered them daily at the hour of prayer, and obtained, when alone, the evidence that her prayer was heard, and that her instructions would be blessed. She invited her class to come weekly to her room, that she might pray with them, and enforce the truths she taught upon the Sabbath. And how glorious was the result.

"She truly loved and sought to do good While thus laboring in the Sabbath school, she was also in the habit of relieving as far as possible the poor and destitute, and imparting to them religious instruction."

In a letter to her sister, written at this time, she mentions, among other things, her visits to a colored family, whom she found desirous of receiving spiritual instruction, though in a very destitute condition, as to things of this life.

"Such an abode of human beings, dear L——, I never saw before—so wretched, so uncomfortable, so replete with suffering and revolting to nature! I could not but feel that this was in some faint degree like what I must expect to meet, that *such beings* were to be my companions and neighbors, *such* abodes my frequent and only resort, and such employment to fill my heart and hands, but still I do not shrink. No! no! dear sister, *if ever I panted for Missionary toil, it was while under that wretched roof*, and I could say from my heart, much as I love you, dearest, much as I love my good, my precious, invaluable *mother*, my brothers, and other relatives, I would not, I *could* not give up the privilege of toiling, of *suffering even*, for souls like these; for 'when I come to stretch me for the last in unattended agony, on India's burning sand, it will be sweet that I have toiled for other worlds than this. I know that I shall feel happier than to die on a softer bed.' Yes, I felt a sweet satisfaction and pleasure in anticipation of the future, while I was talking to poor M——. O it was cheering to see the big tears roll down her dark face as she listened to the tale of a Saviour's love; how happy shall I be, if I am permitted to meet her ransomed spirit, made white in the blood of the Lamb, and sing with her in our heavenly abode, 'Worthy the Lamb.'"

Again she writes thus:

"I have just returned from a walk much exhausted, but have passed a most delightful afternoon;—have called on twelve or fifteen families, and some of them miserable beyond description. O L——, you can have no idea of the wretchedness we have witnessed; there is nothing in B. to be compared with it; this is truly heathen ground. I feel that I need two bodies when I behold such degradation and ignorance in *our favored land.*

"I could easily wear out one short life here in Missionary toil, as well as in Burmah. But, O my sister! I am so entirely unfit to engage in so glorious a work, my heart is so depraved, I *tremble when I think of taking upon myself the responsible duties of a Christian Missionary.* I have before *known* and in some degree felt that I was altogether unholy; but *never* until recently have I discovered my deep pollution of soul, *never* have I had such views of my great guilt as it must appear in the eyes of a Holy God. I could almost wish to hide myself from the view of any human being until I can be more like what I ought.

"My heart seems the depository of every evil, and I cannot endure *to be near myself.* O could I be free from the body of sin, how light would be my load. I have in times past taken pleasure in *finding myself sensible* of my guilt. I rejoiced that I could *feel* and *hate* it; but to be the subject of *so much sin,* so much self loathing, is indeed painful. But I must not burden you, dear L——, with my tale of guilt. I must carry it to the foot of the cross; there only can I hope to lose it. I will only beg an interest in your addresses at the throne of grace, that God would keep me from wounding his cause. I used to look forward with high pleasure to Missionary labor, and think it would have a tendency to wean my affections from earth, and make me more holy. I have, I fear, been depending upon this broken reed, and I now feel that *it may be* the Lord has marked my calculations, has withered my vain hopes, and is now leaving me to *myself*, to show me my error, my weakness, and thus to sweep away the refuge of lies. O I do feel that although he leaves me for a time, he will return again when he has fully shown me my nothingness, my entire dependence upon himself. O L——, what an awful thing it is to be *left* to ourselves! I can imagine no state more awful; I fully believe I have not a worse enemy than *self;* it is my earnest prayer that God would deliver me from this worst evil."

It is doubtful if any stronger or more correct impression can be obtained respecting persons, than by perusing letters written by them in the fullness of the heart's emotions, and penned for the perusal of one friendly eye alone: the heart's sincere and free outpourings, without so much as being crossed by the shadow of a thought that in after years they might be laid open to public view. In unrestrained epistolary correspondence, where there is so much warmth of feeling and noble frankness as the letters of Mrs. C. exhibit, we have far clearer conceptions of the character we contemplate, than can be received from the finest observance of actions, or the most ingenious conclusions drawn from externals alone.

It is *herself* we read as we peruse the lines her hand indited; we seem to be near her, nay more, to catch the very sound of her voice. A genuine letter is to the mind, what a faithfully executed portrait is to the eye, and brings the author into an existence as attractive if not as absolute as was the real.

We will give one more extract from Mrs. Comstock's letters while at Hamilton. The following was written toward the close of her residence there. After giving a description of the Missionary School, so called, which she was attending, and of her interest and proficiency in the study of the Burmese language, she remarks with reference to her anticipated future.

"Should we never *all* meet again on earth, I hope we shall be prepared to meet around our Father's throne in a heavenly home, where there will be no more sad Farewells.—

I can scarcely realize that the time *is so near* when I shall extend the parting hand to all my loved friends, and forever leave the home of my youth, the scenes of my childhood, and the land of my birth for a heathen home, a Burman hut, among a 'people whose tender mercies are cruel,' but O, I do not regret it. What a privilege to be permitted to go forth to the wretched votaries of Gaudama, with the proclamation of peace through a Saviour's blood, to raise the candidates of a cheerless 'Nigban' to bright hopes of immortality! Every day the work before me increases in magnitude, and each day enhances its glory.

"Ah! surely I am of all persons unworthy of such a high honor! How destitute of that deep soul-sustaining piety that I so much need! How little love do I manifest for my Saviour! How little self-denial am I willing to exercise! These things, my dear M——, and these only, cast a gloom over the future. If ever I feel sad in anticipation of the scenes before me, it is not that I am so soon to part *forever* with my beloved friends, not that I leave the home of youthful joys,—

the scenes of my childhood, and the companions of my earliest days,—the sharers of my pleasures and griefs, for an humble home among the rude and barbarous Burmans. No! I can spend my days more pleasantly in my bamboo shed, in pointing idolaters to Jesus, than if surrounded by all the pomp and splendor of civilized and refined society. But dark thoughts of my deep sinfulness oft wring my soul with grief. It is this that prompts the heavy sigh as I cast my eyes forward and glance at the responsibility of my station. O will you not remember me in your supplications at the mercy seat."

Such were some of the exercises of Mrs. C.'s mind during her stay in Hamilton; and afterward when at home, while preparations were in course for her departure, she manifested the same spirit of humility, entire consecration to the service of God, and unwavering determination in the cause in which she had embarked. Serene and happy amid the tearful regrets of those from whom she was soon to separate, she showed how the true Christian can triumph over natural affection and leave behind objects and scenes dear as life itself, at the voice of duty—the call of God. Ah! it was not that she loved her friends and kindred little, it was because she loved Jesus more. None possessed deeper, stronger emotions of friendship, to none could natural ties be more dear. But the language of her heart was, "Here, Lord, I give them all away," and Divine love made the sacrifice a cheerful, willing gift.

The services which occurred on the evening when Mr. and Mrs. Comstock, with other Missionaries, were publicly set apart and instructed as to their future course, were of deep and thrilling interest. They were held on the evening of the 29th of June, 1834, in the Baptist Meeting House, in Baldwin Place, Boston.

On that occasion the Rev. Dr. Wayland delivered a fervent and impressive address to Grover S. Comstock, William Dean, Justus H. Vinton, Hosea Howard, and Seawall M. Osgood, with their wives, and Miss Ann. P. Gardner.

Many a tear fell in that vast congregation assembled to witness the solemn scene, and many a heart throbbed with strong emotion in view of those disciples of Jesus, who thus openly gave themselves to the work of bearing to lands of moral darkness the glorious light of the Gospel.

The closing portion of Dr. Wayland's address was in the following language:

"And now, Missionary brethren and sisters, we bid you adieu. God speed you on your way to your stations. If you fail, a darker night than they have yet seen will brood over Burmah, Siam, and the Islands of the Sea. But the Spirit of Him that raised Christ from the dead, dwelling in you, you will not fail. Glory, such as eye hath not seen, nor ear heard, nor the heart of man conceived, awaits you. When the throne shall be set, and the books opened, and the dead shall be judged out of the things written in the books, then shall ye present before the face of Him that sitteth on the throne, a multitude which no man can number, who have washed their robes, and made them white in the blood of the Lamb, saying, 'Lord, here are we, and the children whom thou hast given us.' And as those myriads purified from all the pollutions of sin, shall, while the ceaseless ages of eternity roll on, become more and more resplendent in holiness, ye who have been wise shall shine as the brightness of the firmament, and ye who have turned many to righteousness, as the stars forever and ever.

"And now, may the God of all grace, who hath called you to his eternal glory by Christ Jesus, make you perfect, stablish, strengthen, settle you: to whom be glory and dominion forever and ever. Amen. Brethren and sisters, *Farewell.*"

The scene of the embarkation of these Missionaries was of no less intensity of interest than that of their public consecration. They were intending to sail the day following, but in consequence of a prevailing fog and head winds, were detained until the second day of July. When the hour arrived, and the last tender parting word had been exchanged, the last embrace given and received, and the ship, destined to waft them over a stormy sea to distant unfriendly homes, had spread her white sails and was receding from the wharf, there came from the little devoted band upon deck, the clear, sweet sound of voices, chanting their farewell in the words of the beautiful Missionary hymn:

"Yes! my native land, I love thee!
All thy scenes I love them well;
Friends, connections, happy country!
Can I bid you all farewell?
Can I leave you—
Far in heathen lands to dwell?"

The following brief note, doubly interesting as being the last words of Mr. and Mrs. Comstock penned within sight of their native land, was conveyed to the friends on shore by the pilot on his returning from the departing ship:

"Ship Cashmere, July 5d, 1834.

"Dear Sister,

"We meet no more on earth, but very soon we shall be in heaven; we do feel as if Christ was with us in the ship, and he will be with you on land. Let us love him with all our hearts, and serve him with all our powers of body and mind. We love our dear friends, but we hope we love Jesus better.

"We shall never forgct you—our best love you have.—Farewell!

"God abundantly bless you, is the prayer of

"Your most affectionate brother and sister,
"G. & S."

Mrs. Comstock's own peculiar feelings on this eventful occasion are best described by herself in a letter penned a year afterwards, in which she reviews the trying scenes of her departure.

"I cannot suffer my eyes to close," she writes, "without holding a few moments' silent, yet sweet converse with those far off but loved friends with whom, just *one year* since, I left for the last time the dear paternal roof. Yes, this is the anniversary of that never-to-be-forgotten day, on which I took a returnless step from my native village, from my home and friends.

"Ah! well do I remember *that day—that last hour*. You know, dear parents, that we met Mr. Comstock on our way to Boston, and I returned with him, and remained about an hour. *That* hour memory has deeply engraved. Even Time's effacing fingers will fail to erase it. It seems as if it were but yesterday that I re-entered the door, from which, with you, I had just come out, as I thought, for the last time, and found all still, silent, and forsaken.

"I sauntered through the house, and at last found S——, seated on the upper stair in tears. She was sole occupant. I took another last look at each room; but all was as the stillness of death. In the south front chamber Mr. Comstock and myself knelt in prayer for the last time. It was during *that* prayer that my feelings for the first time overcame me, in view of the trying scenes before me. But the conquest was momentary. A thought of the shortness of time, the wretchedness of the heathen, and the dying love of *their* and *my* Saviour, soon restored tranquillity and peace.

"I next went into the north front chamber, that place which had so often been a Bethel to my soul. As I gazed about the room, my eyes fastened upon one chosen spot, in which my Saviour had often deigned to bless me with his presence. And while I thought of the many delightful hours spent there in pleading for my dear Sabbath school class, brothers, the heathen, and for a knowledge of the divine will in relation to my future life, I could scarcely forbear uttering the words of the poet:

'To leave my dear friends, and from kindred to part,
To go from my home, it affects not my heart,
Like the thought of absenting myself for a day
From that blessed retreat where I've chosen to pray.'

"Yes, dear parents, that was a *chosen retreat;* and it was not without a struggle that I was enabled to leave it.

"While I stood, silently and sad, musing on the past, the thought occurred that—

'My Saviour resides everywhere.
And can in all places give answer to prayer.'

Then I threw myself upon my knees, and alone once more offered a farewell petition 'with thanksgiving;' and forever left a spot dearer to me than a' cthers in my native land."

O was there no sacrifice felt in the departure of these servants of God? Was there none on the part of the near kindred who returned homeward sorrowing; the mother, who, for the Saviour's sake, took the treasure that lay so close to her heart, and committed it to the winds and waves, that it might be borne a shining light to a dark and far off world? Let the recording angel answer, when God shall give to those who have made sacrifices for Him in this world, a hundred fold in that which is to come.

CHAPTER IV.

Glance at the destined land—Voyage to Amherst—Letters written on ship-board—Extracts from Journal—Joy in suffering—Sabbath at Sea—Arrival—Pagoda worship—Visit to the grave of Mrs. Ann H. Judson—Arracan.

O waft me to that distant shore—
From whence my feet shall come no more;
My only home henceforth shall be
Where'er the Lord hath work for me.

It will be interesting here, perhaps, to glance for a few moments at that far off portion of the world, destined to be the future home of the expectant Missionaries.

Mr. and Mrs. Comstock had been appointed by the board as laborers in Arracan. Originally this province was a part of the Burman Empire, but since 1826 has been in the possession and under the government of the East India Company. It lies on the easterly side of the Bay of Bengal, south of Chittagong and between 15° 54′ and 20° 51′ north latitude. It is divided for government purposes into four principal districts the

Akyab, the Ramree, Aeng, and Sandoway, of these Akyab is the most important, the Ramree district which is an island being second to this. The station intended for Mr. and Mrs. Comstock was Kyouk Phyoo at the north point of Ramree island.

At this period the province of Arracan, with a population estimated at 250,000, was favored with but one Missionary, the Rev. I. C. Fink, sent out by the Serampore Society. His station was in Akyab north of Ramree, and at a considerable distance from it. Aeng and Sandoway were entirely destitute of Missionary laborers.

The inhabitants of Arracan consist of various races, of which the earliest and principal are the Mugs. The others are Burmese, Musselmans, Kyens, Bengalese, Toungmroos, Kemees, and Karens. This variety, of course, occasions a corresponding variety of religious modes of life and manners, some being more deeply steeped in ignorance and superstition than others, but all in the utmost need of the purifying and enlightening influences of Christianity—a nation sitting in darkness in the region and shadow of death, among whom but a faint light as yet had sprung up.

The Missionaries sailed from Boston in the ship Cashmere, on the 2d of July, 1834, and after a voyage of five months they reached Amherst on the 6th of December. The voyage was made up of the usual complement of fair and rough weather, sea-sickness and the various trivial incidents that occasionally break the monotony of sea-life. So far as possible, they employed their time in religious exercises and preparations for the future. Often their hearts reverted to the dear friends and scenes left far behind; always with keen affection, but never with regret. As week succeeded to week, their love for the souls of the perishing heathen grew stronger, and their desires increased to commence their heaven-directed toil. They also received the continued assurance that they were in the path of duty, and often consecrated themselves anew to Him who had called them to labor in his vineyard, desiring to be wholly his for his own high and holy purposes.

Let us present here an extract from a

letter written by Mrs. C. to a dear friend in America, a few weeks before landing; it is dated,

"Ship Cashmere, Bay of Bengal, Nov. 15, 1834.

"MY VERY DEAR S—,

"One hundred and thirty-six days since, at this very hour, I waved you a smiling, yet sad adieu, and I am yet with the remainder of the Missionary band caged in our floating home on the bosom of the mighty deep. I well remember, and can never forget, my dear S——, your last words to me upon leaving home :—'You look happy!'—I *felt* happy, not because I had forever parted from my beloved friends. No!—*that hour* was one of bleeding anguish to friendship and affection, and well nigh proved their death-stroke. But they survived the shock to flourish with tenfold vigor. I find my love for you and other dear American friends, like Goldsmith's length'ning chain—it augments its weight every step I recede from the object of its attraction. But I felt happy, because I was conscious of being in the path of duty, and of doing the will of my

Heavenly Father. I felt too, that the pain I was enduring, and involuntarily causing endeared friends to endure, would be temporary, and would be cancelled by the joy that even one ransomed Burman,—made happy, through our instrumentality, would feel through eternity.

"Our voyage, thus far, has been as comfortable as could be expected. We have much to be grateful for. My greatest cause for gratitude is the sickness which I have been called to suffer; I humbly hope it has been the means of reclaiming my wayward heart from the snares of sin into which it had strayed. While you were at B., and at the time of my departure, I was comparatively in a cold, lifeless state, as far as religion was concerned, and but for the timely chastisement of my Heavenly Father, I might have continued thus. Now I desire to 'redeem the time;' I wish, henceforth, to be wholly the Lord's,—to wear out my life in his glorious service. I can adopt as mine the language of the poet,—

'I want not India's pearly shore,
I want the joys of earth no more,

I want to quit each vain delight,
I want to walk with Christ in white.

I want to know my Saviour's love,
I want to fix my heart above,
I want more grace to conquer sin,
I want to feel new life within.'"

Again she writes thus to her sister, a few weeks after leaving port:

"Ship Cashmere, July 28th.

"MY DEAR, VERY DEAR SISTER,

"*Sister!* what a charm has that word to my ears! I do not know that the second of July imparted to it any *new* power; but since that time, its sound penetrates my soul with peculiar force. I think I feel grateful that God has given me so deservedly dear a sister. It is true, dearest L——, we are separated from each other, but when I contemplate the *end* of our earthly pilgrimage, it seems but a momentary sundering of fond hearts. O how sweet, *passing* sweet will it be, loved sister, when we have toiled out life's remnant *to die*—and *go home* and meet where no farewells will rend the sacred ties of sisterly love. We will henceforth strive to devote each hour to the cause of our blessed Saviour, and heed not toil, suffering, or self-denial,—for each pang endured for Christ's sake, will only add a new gem to our heavenly crown."

During her sea-voyage, Mrs. Comstock kept an interesting journal of each day's occurrences, in which also from time to time she touches upon the religious exercises of her mind, and the corresponding feelings of the other Missionaries; and frequently breathes warm and earnest aspirations after the work to which she was hastening. She suffered greatly from sea-sickness and its accompanying discomforts, yet her spiritual enjoyments continued with her through all the tedious way, and she bore her trials and privations without a murmur or regret. She looked upon it as a necessary part of a Missionary's lot, needful to be endured in order to make the heathen acquainted with the way of life.

At one time, in describing the state of her health to her mother, she makes use of the following language:

"I hope my dear Parents will not infer from what I have written, that I am discontented or unhappy, *for I really am not.* I was never happier in my life. That we have trials and some hardships, which call for the exercise of patience and fortitude, I *will not pretend to deny.* But these trials are much less than I anticipated, and I feel pleasure in submitting to all that my Father sees fit to inflict, that we may give the Bible to the perishing millions of Burmah. If *suffering* is a *prerequisite* to the emancipation of the heathen from the thraldom of superstition and idolatry,—I am willing to *suffer* as long as life lasts, to accomplish my part of the work, for I feel that my happiness is intimately connected with that of this degraded, wretched people. Trials and hardships I expected, when I decided to devote my poor, feeble efforts to the cause of degraded Burmah;—and thus far I can say, I feel sincerely grateful for privations, because they enable me more fully to appreciate the blessings I have enjoyed. How very little of real gratitude did I ever feel in America for the every-day comforts and blessings of life with which

I was favored. How very little value, comparatively speaking, did I place upon these blessings—yet without them I have found more enjoyment since I came on board ship, from the exercise of *gratitude* than I ever experienced from *possessing* them.

"With regard to my sickness, I feel *most* grateful to my Heavenly Father for afflicting me. Mercy has been mingled with chastisement, and I can say, 'it is good for me that I have been afflicted.'

'All I meet I find assists me,
In my path to heavenly joy,
Where, tho' trials now attend me
Trials never more annoy.'"

Again her Journal reads thus.

"The heat during last week has been very oppressive, insomuch that we ventured on deck only at evening after sunset. At night the air is very much confined in our little state room, so as to banish sleep almost entirely. The only relief I can find is in constantly turning myself and my pillow from one side to the other, and even then,—

'It is but poor relief I gain,
To change the place, but keep the pain.'

"And now, methinks, my dear parents are ready to ask, Is not Sarah satisfied with a Missionary life? Is she not *now* willing to return to her happy home—to the bosom of her friends—to the pleasures, conveniences and luxuries of civilized life? But my beloved parents, *dear as you are to my heart*, and highly as I prize these enjoyments; much as I value personal ease, and deprecate privation, I can give but one, and that a hearty answer, No! No! I do not, I can not, regret that I have entered on a life of toil and suffering for the sake of the poor heathen. When I have been suffering *most*, the work before me has appeared even *more* delightful, and the souls of the heathen *more* precious if possible, than during that hour which reported in heaven, my first solemn consecration of myself and mine to the cause of Burmah; and I have felt an indescribable *peace*, yea, *joy* in suffering for its sake. You know, my dear parents, I felt an assurance that *God directed* me to take the step I *did* take, on the evening of the first of January, 1833, and that this was the abiding conviction of my heart, while I remained with you. I am sure nought but a *full*, forcible conviction that I was doing the will of my Heavenly Father *could* have supported—yea *cheered* me during that never to be forgotten hour, in which I waved a last adieu to beloved friends, to you, my dear parents, and my brothers and sisters—and smiled a long and last 'farewell' to my native hills; and this same feeling has been my consolation on board ship, while 'tossing to and fro unto the dawning of the day.'"

At another time when nearing the expected port, she thus expresses herself.

"Monday, Nov. 17. Yesterday was the sacred Sabbath. I went on deck all day to attend worship; in the morning brother D—— preached, and in the afternoon Mr. Comstock spoke from Jeremiah 17, 9. It will probably be his last sermon on board the Cashmere, as three weeks will elapse ere it comes his turn again, but we hope that three weeks from yesterday will find us worshiping in the Zayat with redeemed Burmans. I think yesterday was the happiest day of my sojourn on board ship. I have not before enjoyed so sweet and intimate communion with heaven—have not found as near access to the Throne of Grace, nor felt as deeply for the poor heathen.

"Mr. C—— mentioned in his prayer the wide contrast that existed between us and the perishing Burmans;—that while *we* were bowing before the only living God, and worshiping the Saviour of the lost, they were paying homage to senseless idols. I do not know that I ever realized so deeply before, *my* high privileges, or *their* awful degradation; and when I thought, that *ours* was destined to be the high privilege of giving them the precious Bible, and of introducing the Babe of Bethlehem to their lowly and cheerless huts, and moreover, that we were already *so near* to the full fruition of these our *brightest earthly hopes*, I could not repress tears of heart-felt gratitude—mingled, I hope, with some degree of humility. O my dear parents! *do* you not, and *will you not continue* to mingle your thanksgivings with ours, for the delightful privileges conferred upon your unworthy children?"

On another occasion we find Mrs. C., pacing the desk in the early morning, watching the light as it begins to break forth from the east.

"It seemed," she says, "a fit emblem of the Gospel day which has just begun to dawn upon the natives of the Orient. O that the Sun of Righteousness might arise on them with healing in his beams, and shine with his mighty power until every soul shall be illuminated!"

Again, she remarks, "O I am happy, and long to be where I am to labor. If bliss can be found on earthly soil, I think it will be bliss to live, toil and die for the poor Burmans, and then to meet them in heaven."

This is strong language, but it was the heart's true expression, and, that it sprung from no transient glow of enthusiasm, was clearly proved by the fact, that when in after years she had fairly entered upon the toils of Missionary life, she shrank not from them; her joy and rejoicing still continued, and her love and devotion remained to the end.

Upon the conclusion of their voyage, the Missionaries spent a short time at Amherst, after which they proceeded to Maulmain.

While at the former place, Mrs. C. witnessed for the first time religious services performed in the Pagodas, or places of heathen worship, and she thus describes her feelings on this occasion.

"If ever my face was crimsoned by shame, or my heart smitten with remorse, it was, when I turned from the display of devotion and zeal, made by poor deluded wretches to their unconscious god—and looked upon the abodes of poverty and misery in which they were content to dwell, that they might erect a more splendid habitation for their object of worship. O, thought I, if American Christians, (*I* felt myself unworthy that sacred name,) did but feel and manifest as much love and devotion to the 'High and Holy One, who dwelleth not in the temples made with hands,' how soon should we behold the houses of the living God, towering on the site of these demolished temples!"

At Amherst also, Mrs. C. visited the grave of the sainted Mrs. Ann H. Judson, whose remains rest peacefully beneath the shade of the far-famed Hopia tree.

"Though I mention it last," she writes,

MRS. JUDSON'S GRAVE.

"it was the first place we visited. You cannot imagine, for I cannot describe, the feelings which agitated my breast as I leaned over the dilapidated railing which enclosed the mouldering dust of this sainted woman. *I felt to consecrate myself anew* to that cause, in which she met a Christian martyr's glorious death.

During their residence at Amherst and Maulmain, Mr. and Mrs. Comstock employed themselves in studying the language of the country, and preparing to enter into a permanent field of labor in some one of the provinces of Arracan. This section of the country, at that time, was not only destitute of religious teachers, but was reputed as very unhealthy, especially for foreigners. But there was no hesitancy on their part to enter this uninviting region. It was enough for them to know that hundreds and thousands were living and dying there without a knowledge of a Saviour who died for their redemption. Trusting in the Lord, they went boldly forward, and leaving Amherst and Maulmain, departed for Kyouk Phyoo, a town in the northern part of Ramree island.

CHAPTER V.

Arrival at Kyouk Phyoo—Temporary home—Anxiety to labor—The work commenced—Manners and habits of the Arracanese—Letters to her Parents—to a Christian Physician—and to the church at Brookline.

> Strange scenes the heathen world displays,
> Where Boodh his mighty sceptre sways,
> And men, to gods of wood and stone,
> Bow in their sinful blindness down;
> Yet souls immortal here abide,
> For whom the Lord of glory died.

THE Missionaries arrived in Kyouk Phyoo on the 4th of March, 1835, and, until a permanent residence could be arranged for them, they were kindly received into the house of Mr. Adams, at that time master intendant of the port. This gentleman treated them with great cordiality and attention, and strove to induce them to remain in his family until the rainy season should be over, alleging that they would be much more comfortable than elsewhere. But he urged his hospitable plea in vain; they were too anxious to locate themselves as soon as possible, where their usefulness could be decidedly felt.

Let us read Mrs. C.'s own sentiments in view of this proposal. She says, "Mr. A—— has been extremely kind to us since we have been here, and is very desirous that we should stay with him through the rains; he says he shall be most happy to do any thing in his power for us, and we shall have all of one side of his house partitioned off for us, if we like; and, as another reason why we *ought* to stay, he says the little school-house will be very uncomfortable, and then *we have no servants.* O! how little does he appreciate the motives that induced us to leave our native land and dear friends. How little does he know of the feelings of our hearts! I suppose there are some in our native land, perhaps even among our dear friends, who would think us *fortunate*, and feel that we should gladly accept such an offer. But *no!* nothing could be more foreign to our wishes. His house would be a prison to us, were we obliged to remain in it. So much show, expense, and equipage, would but ill coincide with our feelings, or the object we have in view. No; we came to India expecting a life of toil and hardship; we were prepared for self-denial and suffering. We left our beloved friends, *only* that we might labor for the souls of dying heathen, and shall we be drawn aside from our purpose for the sake of ease and luxury? Shall we consent to live where the poor heathen would be excluded, or considered intruders? No! give me the little bamboo hut amid the natives, and give me a tongue to tell them of Jesus, and I'll ask no more. O, how I long to be engaged in the happy work!"

There was much truth in the remark of Mrs. C——, that this gentleman did not know or appreciate the motives by which the Missionaries were actuated in persuading them to remain quiet during the rainy season. It is difficult for the worldly heart that has never known the exceeding love of God as the renewed soul perceives and feels it, to comprehend the kindred affection the Missionary has for his perishing fellow men, when, to do them good, he is willing to practise self-denial, and endure long privation and suffering. To such a one, the burning zeal of a servant of God appears but the intense devotion of an enthusiast,—the offspring of a generous philanthropy, that has been nurtured and cherished until it has become a nucleus that has gathered to itself all the emotions and energies of the soul. It is a noble thing to accomplish good for time, but it is nobler to toil for benefit that shall be eternal. To one who believes and feels the truth of this, moments are precious and delays sources of regret.

As soon as practicable, therefore, Mr. and Mrs. Comstock were settled in their new but humble home, where they were only too thankful to be visited by the poor degraded heathen, that they might tell them the way of salvation.

At this station (Kyouk Phyoo) they remained a little more than two years, laboring in various ways for the spiritual benefit of this destitute people.

A great part of this province is mountainous, and much is jungle or uncultivated land. The people live in small villages scattered over the surface of the country; consequently, it was necessary for Mr. C—— to perform much itinerant labor in the vicinity as well as in Kyouk Phyoo. This carried him often from home into various scenes and places, where he scattered little tracts, like way-side seed sown in hard and unfruitful soil. Mrs. C—— remaining chiefly in Kyouk Phyoo, where she organized a school for boys, imparting instruction in English and Burman.

The following letter, written at this time by Mr. C——, is interesting from its graphical description of the manners and scenes of their new country and home. It is addressed to a sister of Mrs. Comstock.

"Kyouk Phyoo, April 24, 1835.

"My dear Sister,

"I doubt not that your imagination often busies itself in endeavoring to present to your view our situation as it really is, but its efforts are all in vain. There is nothing in America with which things in India can be compared. Nature here puts on an aspect different from any which she has ever presented to your view. The habits of the people, etc., are as peculiar to the country as is its natural scenery. Now, during the hot season, it appears as if burning sands, and sterile wastes were the principal characteristics of the region about us. Several stately trees are in sight of our house, but they have not the plenteous and rich foliage of similar trees in America. In a *jungle* (a parcel of uncultivated land) near us, stunted shrubs and wild vines cover much of the ground. We have no pleasant groves, and but few indifferent gardens. Well, say you, this is rather a sorry scene; but were you here, it would strike you as being so much in consonance with the climate, etc., that you would not regard it as singular, or at all out of place.

"A native village is just in front of our house. The houses are generally raised some four or six feet from the ground, their average height from the floor to the ridge-pole is eight or ten feet, and they are fifteen, twenty, or twenty-five feet square. Under, or in them, are the men, women, and children, as well as all their domestic animals. The sleeping, cooking, eating, and sitting are all done in one room. As they have no fire-places or chimneys, the houses sometimes smoke. The natives are much smaller than Americans, and cannot do more than a quarter of their work. This, however, is, I think, one of the unavoidable effects of a hot climate, and, one for which a God of wisdom and benevolence has provided, by giving the inhabitants a comfortable subsistence at the expense of very little hard labor. The food is rice and other vegetables, with fish occasionally. The dress of men is a piece of cloth, three or four yards long, wrapped round the middle, with another smaller one wrapped around the head. The women dress rather more, and the children, under seven or eight years of age, not at all. Almost all are very slovenly and dirty in their appearance. They do not appear as intelligent as the inhabitants of America; but how much of this is to be ascribed to natural causes, I cannot say; I think, however, that true religion, and true science would do much to remove it. The people are all lazy, working only when they cannot well avoid it. They are very much attached to the customs of their fathers.

"All their communication between places at any distance from each other is by water. This circumstance, with that of their frequent bathings, renders the people almost amphibious. Till a person has been a short time in the country, many things seem strange which in a little while become familiar and natural. If you sail in a boat, you are carried to and from it on the shoulders of men. If you ride out on a pony, a servant must follow, to hold the horse and assist you to mount or dismount, if needful. If you ride on an elephant, which is very customary with foreigners here, of course a servant strides his neck to guide him, and frequently others follow. It is much more comfortable and pleasant, riding on an elephant, than one would imagine without a trial. I have neither pony nor elephant, but through the politeness of friends have rode on both, and of course have done so in the English style. The palanquin, or tonjon, which is a vehicle borne on men's shoulders, I have not yet tried.

"Few of the English officers carry their own umbrellas, if they happen to walk out in the sun; or if they walk out when there is no sun, they are seldom attended by less than two servants. These fashions, as you would suppose, are not followed by the Missionaries. I have now almost filled a letter with a description of things here, and I fear your ideas respecting them will not be much more definite or correct after you have read it, than they were before.

"If you think I have devoted too much time and space to these things, I can only say that my aim has been to gratify a curiosity which I deem innocent. I know and feel that the interest of the Missionary and of Christians at home, should be in the religious state of the heathen. On this subject I have as yet very little of interest to communicate. The religion of the Arracanese is the same as that of the Burmans, Boodhism, and it is indeed a most desolate system. I have not as yet found the man who could speak with any kind of confidence in reference to his state beyond the grave. All say, when closely pressed, that they know not where they shall go, when they die. O that they were wise and would accept the proffered mercy!

"Their attention to religious instruction is very encouraging, but they are very dark, and need 'line upon line, precept upon precept.' I frequently have opportunities of talking to assemblies of six, ten, twenty or thirty, and Mrs. C—— has quite a number of female visitors. Our location is a good one, and I feel some gratitude, I trust, that God has given me the privilege of laboring here. I want more faith, love, and zeal; for these, strive together with me in your prayers."

It cannot here be uninteresting to know, from her own pen, in what way Mrs. Comstock spent her time, and what were the feelings which agitated her bosom in the earlier stages of her Missionary career. Here is a letter which will instruct us in these matters.

"Kyouk Phyoo, Feb. 22, 1836.

"MY BELOVED PARENTS:

"Though wearied by the duties of the day, I sit down at ten o'clock to write you a few lines. I am alone, at the Mission Cottage, as Mr. C. is residing a few weeks in the destitute region of Ramree, employed in preaching Christ, and distributing tracts. From morning until after dark, I have been constantly employed to-day, in telling the multitudes of heathen who have crowded around my door, of the love of Jesus to dying Arracan. For a week past, there has been an increase of inquirers, but this day has surpassed all others. I have scarcely had time to eat. Nor have I felt any appetite for earthly food; my soul has been satisfied with meat which the world knows not of. My congregations to-day were chiefly composed of men; and among them not a few whose furrowed brows, and silver locks proclaimed them ripe for the grave! O that I might add—for the joys of Paradise! But, alas, they reject that precious—only name by which they can be saved. They have listened attentively, however, to the story of the cross, and begged for 'a book which would tell them about this Jesus Christ, who pities sinners.'

"This has not been the case with all, however. One assembly of about a dozen young men came and sat down with a haughty air, which told me they had come to *sneer*. I verily felt for their souls, and tried to tell them, respectfully and affectionately, that for *them*, a precious Saviour bled and died. But the curling lip, and sullen silence with which they listened, showed that they scorned the message. As I was saying, 'God is a *holy God*, heaven a *holy place*, and no unholy being can dwell there; therefore, Jesus Christ so loved sinful men, that he left the glory and happiness of heaven, and came, and endured suffering, poverty, and death, to atone for their guilt and save them from hell'—as I uttered this sentence, one young man rose in a state of rage, and with a single expression of his displeasure, left, and the others immediately followed. I said, 'Will you take a book, and examine, that you may ascertain the truth?' Some did not reply, but walked haughtily away; others said, 'We don't want your books.'

"For a few moments I felt somewhat dejected, but soon recollected, that nothing but the influences of the Holy Spirit could convert those who had promised most, and *that Power* was adequate to the transformation of even the most obdurate heart. This inspired new courage, and I soon had another large assembly of old men, who listened, for the *first time*, to tidings of an Eternal God, and our Almighty Saviour. These remained until after dark; and this evening, I have been employed two hours in instructing a little boy and Rakaing man who live in my family. The latter came in, saying, 'he very much desired to listen to my words respecting the Eternal God, and his excellent Son; because his eyes were so poor that he could not see to read, and he wanted to know the truth.' Since that time, I have had to attend to domestic affairs a little; and this is the first moment of leisure I have had. This has been truly *a happy day*.

"Language fails to describe the anguish I endured when called to part from my beloved home,—from you, my revered parents, and the endeared ones I had so long and fondly loved. But I must say, *one day* of such sweet, heavenly toil as this, more than compensates for *all*. Yes, let me here labor and die in such a cause, and I will envy not the affluent, wise, or honorable of this world.

> 'In these deserts let me labor,
> On these mountains let me tell
> How He died.'

"It is too late to write more, and praying that you, my beloved parents, may be wise to win souls to God, and enjoy daily a rich foretaste of heaven, I wish you 'good-night.'"

If it were possible still to doubt whether our friend possessed a true Missionary spirit, we have before us a letter to a relative, a pious physician, which will show how her heart desired others, as well as herself, to labor for Christ, and for the welfare of the bodies and souls of men.

"Kyouk Phyoo, May 8, 1836.

"Dear Cousin W——,

"Many thanks for your's of July 20, 1835; it was read with pleasure and gratitude. Its *brevity* was its only fault. I have much that I wish to say in reply, but have a mere fragment of time for writing; you will therefore pardon the liberty I take in telling you freely the thoughts which have often, very often, presented themselves to my mind respecting you, since I have been in this country. When I have looked around on the poverty, degradation, and wretchedness, which everywhere meet my view,—when I have thought of the eternity on which the Christless idolaters are daily entering,—when I listen to the cries for 'a Jesus Christ's teacher' which are wafted to us from every part of this populous, but destitute province; the inquiry has involuntarily risen, Who will pity,—who will come and tell these hundreds of thousands of dying idolaters, of Jesus, the heathen's Saviour? Will no one proffer a morsel of that 'bread of life' which famishing souls so earnestly crave? With these feelings, my thoughts have often been directed to cousin W——; nor could I forbear asking, Why cannot *he* come and teach these benighted wanderers? If you felt it *your duty*, undoubtedly you would do so. But perhaps you have not thought as much on the subject as its importance justifies, or even *demands*.

"You were once settled in business, and

probably considered yourself established for life. But the Lord had other work for you to do; and to prepare you for it, took away your health and your business, and gave you a heart to know and serve Him. You say, when speaking of your future intentions, that your feelings have often led your thoughts towards another profession, but you think you have not there seen the path of duty. Methinks the Lord would say in relation to this, 'It is well that it was in thine heart.' But he has directed your attention to a profession which would tend greatly to enhance your usefulness, should he call you to labor for him among the heathen. I know, my dear cousin, that the talents which God has given you, are such as would enable you to be useful *anywhere;* but could they not be more profitably employed among the poor *Saviourless* heathen, than in a land overflowing with precious, but in many cases, *abused* Gospel privileges?

"You are not aware how *very* useful Christian physicians might be here, and how loud is the call for them. Yet among all the Missionaries of the Baptist Board in India, there is not, I believe *one.* Scarcely a day passes, but we have calls for medical aid; and notwithstanding our almost entire ignorance on the subject, we try to do what we can. Yet we often have cases presented to us, which we cannot, we *dare* not, in our ignorance undertake. O, how would your heart bleed to behold the wretched objects which sometimes present themselves before our door to crave pity, and a little medical assistance! We often feel our blood chilled, and our souls pained by the sight of misery, which it is not in our power to alleviate. I can speak from *observation* only of this place. I *know* that *this* province is in a destitute dying condition.

"But the field is the world! What an encouraging field does *China* present to the philanthropist, the physician, the Christian, and the Missionary! But *where all these are united*, who can calculate the amount of good an individual may accomplish in such a place? Besides this, you can scarcely turn your eye to any part of this eastern world, from which you might not hear a cry for help. Many, many times, before I received your letter, or knew anything of the course you were pursuing, did the thought present itself to my mind, and once or twice I said to Mr. C. 'If cousin W—— would study medicine, and come out as a Missionary, how useful he might be!'

"The receipt of your letter made me feel that your holy mother's prayers would be answered—'that the Lord would make W—— a Christian, and a minister, or a Missionary.' You know something of your mother's feelings towards you, of her ardent affection, and above all, her desire for your *spiritual interests!* On the last point, her feelings, towards the close of her life, were unusually strong. A few days before her death, a Christian friend who called, prayed with her; and I can never forget the expression of her countenance as she thanked her 'for remembering her children.' She was so weak, that she spoke with difficulty, yet she mentioned each of them, and added, while the tears rolled down her emaciated cheeks, 'and there's W——. I think a great deal about him; the Lord has been very good to me and my children; and I have *one desire for him*, and sometimes I feel that the Lord will answer my prayers for him when I am gone.' These were the last words I ever heard her utter on this subject.

"But I return. The cries for a 'Jesus Christ's teacher,' which are coming from every part of this destitute province, and from various other places, *are*, and *must be in vain*, unless Christians in America will pity and come to their aid. And may I not ask you, dear cousin, not to decide to settle down as a physician, in Christian America, without asking your conscience, and your God, whether it be your duty, or not, to come and point these poor idol-worshipers to their God and Redeemer. Do *think* of the millions of souls who have no one to tell them of Him who died to ransom them from hell. Think of them in the light of that day when you will meet them in all their sins, and in all their ignorance of a Saviour's atoning blood, at the judgment-seat. You will think I have used great freedom, but I know you will pardon me. I have witnessed the wretchedness and destitution of these poor souls, and I feel that I must plead for them."

It could not be otherwise than that the members of the church at Brookline, who had felt so intense an interest in the Mission of their beloved sister, and who had presented many fervent prayers on her behalf, should wait with earnest desire to hear from her; and it will be easily imagined that they listened with almost breathless attention to a letter from her own hand, dated

"Kyouk Phyoo, July 3, 1836.

"*To the Baptist Church, Brookline.*

"DEAR BRETHREN AND SISTERS,—

"It is just two years and one month today, since I last sat down with you at the table of our Lord, to commemorate his dying love. Can I ever forget the emotions which agitated my breast at that time? Can I ever forget the many *precious* seasons of 'communion with God,' which I have enjoyed with you in the consecrated place of your Sabbath solemnities; when we have sat under the Saviour's 'shadow with great delight, and found his fruit sweet unto our taste?' Can

I ever cease to love those revered fathers and mothers,—those endeared brethren and sisters,—with whom I first celebrated that holy ordinance? No. Though I may never be permitted to meet you on earth;—though I may no more unite in your sacred Sabbath services, memory will ever delight to dwell on the cherished joys of the past; and this heart must cease its pulsations, ere I cease to love,—ere I cease to pray for the prosperity of that *dear church*, who were the guardians and counsellors of my spiritual infancy, and with whom I *first* found the blessedness of 'denying self,' and 'bearing the cross.' I look back with *deep regret* upon my unfaithfulness, as a daughter, a sister, a Sabbath-school teacher, and as a Christian, while I shared with you the privileges of the Christian Church.

"The sad recollection of all my apathy,—my sinful conformity to the world, has embittered many an hour since I have been deprived of those privileges, and have been so near *a stranger to Christian society*. But Christ came to save the very chief of sinners, therefore, *I* have hope, that from the multitude of my transgressions, his free grace will ultimately deliver me; and that, when the children of the kingdom shall be gathered, from the east and from the west, from the north and from the south, I may again be permitted to join you in our Father's house, and unite with you in an eternal song of praise to 'redeeming grace and dying love.' And, O! shall I not then have the pleasure of introducing to you some of these benighted children of Arracan, who, in answer to your prayers, have been taught the way of life?

"I received a letter yesterday, from our dear pastor, which assured us that we were still remembered in your prayers. And to say that the assurance greatly cheered and encouraged our hearts, would but feebly express our feelings. We have now been widely separated for two years, and I began to feel that we might possibly be forgotten, even by those who so affectionately pledged their payers. But to *know* that we are still remembered, and still have an interest in your intercessions with the Father, greatly revives our spirits, and incites us to renewed ardor in prosecuting our difficult but delightful labor; and may you receive your reward when you meet these now poor deluded idolaters at the judgment seat!

"You will perhaps wish to know how I pass my time,—what are my employments, etc. Our days are spent entirely among the degraded heathen, who care not for 'the living God,' reject the precious Saviour, and despise us as 'the teachers of his law.' We have no Christian associates, with whom to take counsel on the things that relate to our spiritual welfare. There are a few English here, but they seem to care little about real religion, and spend the Sabbath of that God whom they acknowledge with their lips, as if it were no more sacred than other days; and this, too, in the sight of poor, ignorant beings, who judge of the Christian's God only by the conduct of those who profess to be governed by his law. No church-going bell summons us, as formerly, to the assembly of the saints; but we feel the Sabbath to be *a precious privilege*, and we try to spend it profitably.

"Immediately after family worship on Sabbath morning, we meet the children of the two schools, and endeavor to lead their benighted minds to the heathen's Saviour; but it is not like a Sabbath school in a Christian land. It is with the utmost difficulty that we can gain the attention of these ignorant children. An insect or a straw seems to possess greater interest for them than any thing we can say about the blessed Jesus. They hear that the precious Son of God suffered and died on the cross to redeem the little children of Arracan from a dreadful hell, with the most perfect indifference, and even levity. After the Sabbath school we have public worship in the native language; this is attended by few except the schools, and those more immediately connected with us. Occasionally, some passer-by is attracted to the door, where he listens for awhile to the word of life. After native service, Mr. Comstock and myself observe a season of worship in our own house, and once in two months we are permitted to commemorate the dying love of Christ. Though but two solitary individuals, in a heathen land, we are not denied this sweetest of privileges. It has this afternoon been ours, and I have found it truly a refreshing season to my soul. Our humble thatch does not exclude the precious Saviour. He has to-day graciously vouchsafed his presence, and 'his banner over us has been love.' We have found it good to eat and drink in remembrance of His dying love for such sinners as we are. O, may it not be long ere redeemed heathen are sharers with us in this heaven-bought privilege! On Sabbath evenings we have had English worship at our house, principally for the benefit of the drummers and some others connected with the regiment stationed here, who are almost as ignorant as the heathen themselves. They do not feel sufficient interest, however, to attend since the rains commenced, and 'lo! we turn to the heathen.' We shall hereafter devote Sabbath evening to native worship.

"During the week, I spend my time from nine A. M., till three P. M., in the schools. I have daily applications for medicines, and sometimes I am entirely occupied out of school hours in attending to the sick. When any are too ill to come to the Mission-house, I go to their huts, and administer to their wants. The Lord has been very good to us, and has granted us greater success than we, in our ignorance of diseases, had reason to expect. We have frequently been called to treat cases which the native doctors have long and vainly attempted to cure; and as they have been benefited by the treatment received here, we have acquired great influence over them, besides the opportunity of telling them of Christ.

"My paper is filled, and I am compelled to close. I can only add that I find Missionary labor as delightful as I ever anticipated it to be, and rejoice that the Lord has permitted me to leave those dearest to me on earth, and be the messenger of his love to dying heathen.

"That the Lord may be with and bless you, and your beloved pastor, and make you a rich blessing to the world, shall ever be the prayer of one who ceases not to cherish the liveliest interest in the welfare of the little Baptist Church in her native place.

"Affectionately yours, in a precious Saviour,

S. D. C."

CHAPTER VI.

Church constituted in Kyouk Phyoo—Ill health of the Missionaries—Death of Mr. and Mrs. Hall—Earnest plea for the cause of Missions—Increased ill health—Temporary removal to Maulmain—Necessity of relinquishing the station at Kyouk Phyoo—Letter of Mrs. Comstock.

Then trials came, and stern disease,
  That made her oft its prey—
And men from God's own holy word
  Would rudely turn away.
Still undismayed she labored on—
  Nor fear nor doubt deterred;
A faith sublime beheld afar
  The harvest long deferred.

In 1837, on the twenty-first of February, a church was constituted in Kyouk Phyoo. It was composed of the Missionaries, and native assistants, also the wife of one of the latter. Only eight disciples, and a part of these once heathen idolaters, were assembled to commemorate His death, who said, "Do this in remembrauce of me." But they recalled the precious words of their Saviour when he said, "Where two or three are gathered together in my name, there am I in the midst of them;" and though a small and feeble band, they rejoiced in the tokens of his presence, and felt encouraged and strengthened to go forward trusting in Him.

Mr. Comstock recounts this event in his journal as one of great interest. "O may the little church now formed," he says, "be abundantly blessed of God, and soon embrace multitudes of these perishing idolaters."

In the progress of Mr. and Mrs. Comstock's labors in this place, they suffered at intervals much discomfort and sickness from the unhealthiness of the climate. Frequent and sudden changes of weather, combined with unavoidable exposures, seriously affected them. At certain seasons, the atmosphere was decidedly injurious, in consequence of stagnant air given off from marshy places and pools with which the province abounds, occasioning a kind of malaria; this prevails chiefly after the heavy rains, when the rays of a burning sun fall upon the humid soil.

But far more trying to their spirits than any amount of bodily pain and discomfort, was the severe affliction they sustained in the death of Mr. and Mrs. Hall, who had been sent out by the board to aid the Mission at Arracan. They died within a few months of each other of fever common to the country. Fond hopes which were depending on the support and companionship of these beloved fellow-laborers, were thus suddenly cut off; but though the ways of Providence appeared so dark and inscrutable, the Missionaries endeavored to feel that all was right. At such a period, when laborers were so few in Arracan, and the field appeared so vast and important, it was indeed a peculiar and mysterious visitation, but He whose "ways are not as our ways," saw fit to remove his servants thus early to His holier service above.

Says Mr. Comstock on this sad event:

"We deeply feel our loss, but knowing that a kind and wise Father has seen this affliction to be necessary, we bow submissively to His will, and pray that it may be sanctified to our good, and to that of the heathen; and also excite the friends of Missions in America to more vigorous efforts for the extension of Christ's kingdom over the whole earth."

It was about this time that Mrs. Comstock wrote also:

"Shall not our hands be strengthened, and our hearts encouraged ere long by some faithful fellow-laborers from America? Thousands of souls, *precious souls*, who have never heard of a Saviour, of an Eternal God, or an endless hell, are going down to death without a voice of compassion to warn them of their awful doom. O that some of those who profess to love Jesus and His cause, but who yet remain inactive at home, could cast one look on Arracan with her hundreds of thousands of idolatrous sons. If there existed a spark of that love which 'seeketh not her own' in their hearts, pity for the perishing would melt them, and love to Jesus would move them to activity. 'Tis true, these Arracanese do not *themselves* call for help—and why?—Because they are *heathen* as their ancestors have been generation after generation before them. They love their idol gods, and bow down to them in adoration, because they know not that there is a higher, holier Being, than he whom their senseless images represent. Yes, dear, favored sister, it is a heart-rending truth, that there are here, thousands of immortal spirits, precious as our own, who have never heard of One mighty to save, and who are not likely to have the illusions that superstition and idolatry have thrown around them dissipated, save by the light of eternity; unless indeed, some, whom God has blessed with the light of religion, shall feel their hearts touched with pity, and shall cry, '*Lord here am I;* send me to the poor Arracanese, send me to the wandering sons of the mountains, the benighted Kayens.'

"I fear, dear sister, you, and other Christians in America do not feel enough, do not pray enough for the poor heathen, and poor Missionaries, or at least, do not feel in the right way. You need not *feel more* for a Missionary's privations or hardships. They ask not your sympathy, *they need it not in this respect*, but they *do* need your *frequent, fervent prayers*, that they may be more holy and Christ-like, that they may have grace to stem the tide of worldly influence and sin, that deluges this country. Where, even among professed Christians, do we see anything but worldliness, disregard of God's commands, and almost universal daring, shame-faced iniquity? O! how would your heart bleed by a glance at European society in India! I used to feel while in America (I believe it is a rather widely disseminated feeling) that Missionaries should be almost of *necessity*, that they could *scarcely help being* eminently holy; that *holiness* would follow a Missionary life almost intuitively. But since I have seen the influence, almost without exception, *worse* than worldly, by which they are surrounded, I wonder that they are not carried away more, by the error of the wicked; or rather, (for I know there is *no excuse for any one* who is not eminently holy) I am led to praise more loudly that sustaintaining grace, that keeps them from falling and makes them happy in their labors while deprived of the multiplied means of grace they once enjoyed.

"Again, you who are among civilized people, know nothing of the opposition and reproach which a Christian must receive from the heathen; true, there may be some *sunny* spots in the Missionary's career, when they who hear, 'receive the word gladly;' but to how great a majority does the story of a precious Saviour's love seem but an idle tale."

In the second year of their residence at Kyouk Phyoo, the illness of Mr. and Mrs. Comstock became so frequent and severe, that they were obliged to consider the expediency of abandoning the station for a season, until a better degree of health should be given them. This consideration, much to their regret, soon became an imperative necessity, otherwise it became evident their labors would soon cease altogether. Accordingly, they removed at the close of December, 1837, to Calcutta, and from thence to Maulmain, which they reached on the 7th of April, 1838.

They became fully, though sadly, convinced of the necessity of relinquishing Kyouk Phyoo, for a healthier place of permanent residence.

"Of fifty-three Europeans," wrote Mr. C. to the Board, "who have resided there since

I have arrived, some for a few months, and others for two or three years, sixteen have died, nineteen have been seriously sick, some at the very point of death, and two or three others have suffered from sickness; the mortality evidently increases there from year to year." His conclusion in regard to resuming his labors in Arracan, was, that a station should be selected more favorable to health, three of which, Akyab, Ramree, and Sandoway offered themselves for a choice. They felt they should have no hesitation at returning to one of these after the rains were over, and they had recovered their health and strength. Indeed, to use their own language, "Such was the interest they felt in destitute Arracan, they know of no place where they would be more willing to spend the remnant of their days, provided the Mission there should be efficiently sustained by the Board."

At about this period the following interesting letter was written by Mrs. C. to her sister:

"My Beloved Sister,—

"You are probably about to repair to the sanctuary of the Most High, there to join kindred spirits in celebrating the praises of your covenant God, to listen to the voice of admonition, instruction, and encouragement. What a privilege is this you enjoy, my sister! You do not, you cannot realize it. How precious the opportunity you enjoy of growing in grace, and of acquiring that knowledge which will increase your usefulness here, and your happiness above! Often, very often, do I look back with regret upon the many like precious privileges which I have misimproved. How much more holy, more like my Saviour *might* I, *ought* I to have been; how much better qualified for the responsible and difficult station I occupy.

"But the past cannot be recalled. I have *now* only to improve the privileges that remain. Though the hallowed sound of the Sabbath bell may no more salute my ears; though I may never again enter the Sanctuary of the Most High to mingle the voice of prayer and praise with the congregation of the saints, yet ours is a God who will not turn away from the prayer of humble faith, even though it ascend from the lowly bungalow, and we yet enjoy the precious Sabbath, which we may devote more exclusively to His service. Yes, my dear sister, though we are in a heathen land, far, far from those who own and love our Saviour, we have still many privileges, precious privileges, left; and though we feel the loss of the many means of grace to which we were formerly accustomed, if we do not daily make progress in holiness, we shall be without excuse. The Bible, the mercy seat, an omnipotent and merciful God, and an interceding Saviour, are *still ours*, and it is the presence of these that renders a home amid such moral desolation, tolerable, yea, *pleasant*, and makes us happy in our loneliness.

"Notwithstanding the deprivation of the means of grace which we suffer, we would not exchange our lot. No, each month, and week, and day, attaches new importance to this fearfully responsible work in which we are employed, and awakens new compassion for the wretched thousands around us; and were we desired to select a dwelling place from *the face of the whole earth*, *poor*, *degraded*, *desolate Arracan* should be the spot of our choice."

CHAPTER VII.

Mission reopened at Ramree—Church constituted—Extraordinary deliverance—Baptism of Gra Bouck—Varied Labors—Mother's Book—Letter to a brother—Letters to her eldest little daughter on her birth-day—Deep interest in religious intelligence—Anxiety for her own spiritual welfare—Letters.

Ever striving, never weary,
  Healing hearts with sorrow riven,
To those darkened homes, and dreary,
  Bearing radiant beams from heaven;
With a strong heart's deep devotion,
  Thus she still the work pursued,
Evening closed o'er warm emotion,
  Morning light the toil renewed.

For nearly a year the Missionaries continued in Maulmain, and, by the blessing of God, the result of this change was the happy restoration of their much impaired health. In the interval Mr. Comstock was engaged in preaching in various places, distributing tracts, and preparing useful religious books for printing in the Burman language; while Mrs. C. prosecuted her labors of love with untiring zeal, as her enfeebled frame recovered its exhausted powers.

They now desired to return to Arracan, and after some deliberation, they selected Ramree as a place of residence, in consequence of its reputation for salubrity and advantages for successful Missionary labor. They arrived here on the evening of the 10th of April, 1839.

The town of Ramree contained nearly four times the population of Kyouk Phyoo, numbering over six thousand inhabitants. The district of Ramree, including the capital, contained sixty-three thousand. The people appeared to Mr. Comstock to be more intelligent, and willing to be instructed in religious things. Less opposition and apathy were manifested, and labor seemed not without hope.

On the 29th of May, in the same year, Mr. and Mrs. Comstock, together with Mr. and Mrs. Stilson, Missionaries in another section of the district, constituted a church at Ramree, to which was afterwards added seven hopefully converted native assistants who had accompanied them from Maulmain. A small and feeble band, but yet strong in the faith which is in Christ Jesus. Well might Mr. Comstock exclaim, in view of their limited numbers: "O, let not the large and flourishing churches in America forget the little churches just struggling into life in this heathen land."

An extract from a letter addressed in the early part of the following year, by Mrs. Comstock to her mother, will show something of her feelings as a Christian, while it narrates an extraordinary deliverance effected by the good hand of God, in the hour of peril.

"God has indeed been very good to us as a family. I may emphatically say, 'His mercies are new every morning, and fresh every moment.' I have often thought that there is no one who shares more largely in his rich blessings than I do; yet it is too true, that there never was a heart so base, so vile as mine; so faithless to its promises, and so prone to sin.

"Last night we went over to Brother Stilson's, to attend our usual Thursday evening prayer meeting. It was Mr. C.'s turn to lead the exercises of the evening. While he was reading, and remarking on what he read, my thoughts were truant, and I was considering whether the *moon* would be up for us to go home; whether there would be any danger of tigers; and what we should do if one were to jump out upon us, etc., etc. Just then my thoughts were recalled by remarks on the words, 'Fear not, ye are of more value than many sparrows. Are not the hairs of your head all numbered,' etc. I felt reproved for my wandering anxiety, and realized, in some degree, that we could be overcome by no dangers that were not sent by our heavenly Father. Well, we got home safely by the light of a fine, clear moon, and guarded by an unfailing shield. We found L. and O. with their night gowns on, lying under the table, and by their conversation, which we overheard, they were intending to hide themselves from Papa and Mamma. However, as soon as they heard our footsteps, they forgot their design, and came bounding out with pillow in hand to meet us. I immediately took Robert Stearns, and sent my Mug woman off, telling her not to stop to shut the doors, which she usually does.

"After L. O. and R. S. were in bed and asleep, I went into my bathing room, to see if the outside door was shut and tied Between my bed-room, and the bathing room is a narrow passage, in which is placed a stand and basin, or wash-bowl, leaving *merely* room enough to pass through. I had passed the stand, and finding all tied up secure, turned to go back. Just then my eye fell on something which lay coiled up on the wash-stand. It looked like a piece of old cable, and I supposed the children had found it somewhere, and going there to wash their hands, had laid it down. Fortunately I had a light in my right hand. (I had just before been through in the dark.) I held it close to the object, when lo, and behold, the cable turned into a monstrous snake! His quivering tongue was thrust out of his mouth, and with his head erect, he seemed just ready to attack me. His head was not an inch from my arm, and I could not possibly get by him. Fortunately the godown just behind me was ajar. I fled into it, and gave one moan, which was all I had strength to do. It was so sudden a start as to make me quite faint. Mr. C. came with his heavy black cane, which Mr. Vinton obtained and gave him for the Karen jungles, and taking good aim at his head, gave him a more severe shock than he had given me.

"He was six or seven feet long, and the next morning the natives seemed quite horror-stricken when they saw it. When they were told where we found it, they smote their breasts and cried, 'Amah, Amah!'— ['Alas, Alas!'] I asked if it was poisonous, and they replied, 'Hyck helyon tha bo bac;' ['If it bites, it is only for death.'] As soon as I had recovered a little from the shock, I felt again condemned for my faithlessness, and ashamed in view of the *continued* and watchful care and kindness of my heavenly Father, as contrasted with my ingratitude and worldly mindedness."

A different scene follows. The reader cannot but sympathize with this interesting little band in the joy they felt on occasion of their first baptism. Mrs. Comstock thus describes the scene to her mother under the date of April 11, 1842:—"It was an exciting scene here; what would it have been could it have been witnessed in a Christian land? It was on a pleasant Sabbath evening, just at the going down of the sun, that I took Brother Kincaid's arm, and with our children, and numerous natives, followed Mr. C. and the candidate towards the banks of the narrow, but clear pebbly stream, whose meandering course intersects the town. We had scarcely set out before we were stopped by the brother of the candidate, who earnestly warned Mr. C., not to baptize that man. 'He is my brother,' said he, 'and you must take care that you do not break his caste.' Mr. C. told him that it was at the request of his brother that he baptized him, and *he* must take care that he made no disturbance. 'Remember,' said he, 'that there is a law here, and a magistrate to enforce it.' This, probably, intimidated him a little, and he walked quietly on. The number of natives constantly increased around us, all intent on seeing 'some new thing, until we came in sight of Gra Bouck's house. The crowd collected in front, and nearly filled the road. We had fears lest violence should be resorted to, when they found all other efforts fail. They had been striving all the afternoon, by persuasion, entreaties, and threats, to turn away his mind from the faith.

"While yet at some distance from the house, the brother before mentioned came round in front of us, and began to twist up his 'puoo,' very earnestly, in a manner peculiar to these people, when they are angry or about to undertake some wonderful thing Gra Bouck's wife now rushed out from the crowd around the house with disordered hair, and her dress loosely hanging around the lower part of her body. She came running towards us in this plight, brandishing a great plantain-stalk over her head, and yelling out in a most unearthly tone, '*Take care, take care, take care.* Don't you enter this religion!' As soon as she reached us, the shameless woman took hold of her husband's 'puoo,' and began to strip it from him. In this she would have succeeded, had not Mr. C. caught hold of it, and stayed her shameful effort. The brother then tore off his 'goung-boung,' or turban, and snatched away his handkerchief, while his wife laid the plantain-stalk over his back. It was now a most exciting scene. Our children, and Brother K.'s, unused to such sights, began to cry. Gra Bouck's wife, with a countenance pale with rage, except round her mouth and eyes, which were quite purple, was the picture of a very *fiend*. She could not command her natural voice, but with a shrill screaming tone continued to beat Gra Bouck, (except when Mr. C. intercepted the blows by stepping between them) and warned him not to dare to destroy his caste by entering this religion. Then finding her threats of violence lost, she ran before Mr. C., and drawing her hands across her throat, said, 'Here, here, cut my throat.'

"We walked on, as well as the tumult would admit, towards the banks of the clear, still river. When near his house, in the midst of the crowd, Gra Bouck lifted both hands, and, amid the furious tumult, exclaimed, in a full, clear tone, 'All these people I fear not; I fear the Eternal God alone!' After this, there was less disturbance, and we soon reached the baptismal water. An ample bridge across the river, just over our heads, was crowded with people, as also the banks of the river on either side. Now all was still save the buzzing murmur of the thousands of voices around us. While Mr. C. read the solemn baptismal service, and addressed the assembled multitudes, we could see people running from all directions, eager to witness the novel sight.

"It was not decided till noon of the same day when Gra Bouck should be baptized, consequently it could not be extensively known; yet the assembly of people was very large. It was the first time that the solemn ordinance of Christian baptism had ever been administered in Ramree. May it not be the last by very many, that *we* shall be privileged to behold! May it not be long ere these valleys shall again echo to the sweet notes of the solemn and beautiful baptismal hymn!

"The rush to the water side was so furious, that none of us saw the baptism, nor could we scarcely hear the 'I baptize thee in the name of the Father, etc.' All passed off quietly, and as the candidate rose from the water, some one near us called out, 'Tha du, tha du.—['Well done! well done!']

"I cannot tell you, dear mother, my feelings as I stood amid that crowd at the water side,—witnessing this 'first fruits' of Missionary labor in Ramree. It seemed an earnest of a future blessing. And at the same time I could say, if we died without seeing a more abundant blessing, that I could not regret leaving our home and native land. The salvation of even one soul would more than compensate for all. O that the Lord would manifest himself to this devoted city! I believe fully, that many are *convinced.* The *Spirit's* power alone is wanting. Pray, O pray, dear mother, for this richest, best blessing. And may your prayers avail, and bring in a rich harvest of these poor, perishing souls. But for *this hope* of seeing the heathen turn to Christ, life in this country would be an almost intolerable burthen. Such a hope stimulates and animates us. May the Lord help us to have and cultivate the Spirit of Christ in all things, then our labors will not be in vain."

How true it is, that the rising churches, few and weak in heathen lands, need greatly the thoughtful, earnest prayers of their older and stronger brethren on our civilized shores. Our watchcare, and interest, though beginning, should never end at home; but extend beyond the sea into these regions of moral darkness, where Gospel light has but newly come. If grace and strength to resist temptation be needed here, they are doubly needed there to keep the feet from falling, and the heart fixed on the commandments of God.

It was under more favorable auspices that the Mission in Arracan was now re-opened at Ramree, and the Missionaries looked fondly forward with the hope that God would graciously bless their labors, and convert many souls through their instrumentality.

Mrs. Comstock again commenced a school for boys and girls, some of whom made good progress under her instructions. She also loved to gather around her the poor, ignorant females, and tell them of salvation through a crucified Saviour. Her heart bled for their reformation spiritually and morally, as she saw from day to day how the power of Christianity alone can truly elevate our social nature and purify the heart. She saw them as they *were*, crushed and degraded in their dark idolatry; and by the eye of faith she saw them as they *might be*—raised, enlightened and saved, by the triumph of truth over error, and the glorious light of that freedom wherewith Jesus makes us free.

At Ramree, for many years, she taught, labored and prayed. Here she passed through many seasons of trial and suffering, and here also her fainting spirits were often refreshed with manna from on high. She threw into the work her whole soul. With her truly there was no half way. She had laid her all on the altar of God, and no gift was ever withdrawn from the sacred shrine, no talent suffered to slumber, but every energy was aroused to the accomplishment of God's great work among these destitute people. The amount of varied labor which she performed was astonishing. She seems to have sustained at one and the same time, the capacity not only of housekeeper, wife, mother, and school teacher, but that of preacher, physician, and nurse.

In the absence of Mr. C., she herself would tell to those who came to hear, the story of a Saviour's love, and point out the way of salvation. To the sick she would dispense medicines of various kinds, with much sympathy and skill. Her ear was ever open, to the call of the afflicted, and her hand ready to mitigate their suffering. Often would she leave the couch of her own dear little ones, and go to the miserable home of some sick native child, and minister soothingly to the pangs of disease, or close its eyes in death, while her lips would speak to the mourning mother, sweet words of heavenly consolation. She was particularly interested in mothers and little children, and by her gentle sympathy and tender interest in their welfare, she won largely upon the confidence and affections of the dark, ignorant minds by which she was surrounded.

Each day of her life, she sought to accomplish as much good as could be crowded into the limits of its fleeting hours, as though it were the last she might ever see.

Among her other efforts she found time to write two useful little books, entitled "*The*

Mother's Book" and "*Scripture Catechism.*" In the production of the former, she was deeply interested. Such a work in their own language, and adapted especially for their use was greatly needed by the poor heathen mothers.

The following extract from a letter written to her sister while it was in progress, will show how deeply she was absorbed in this labor of love.

"Ramree, Oct. 30, 1841.

"MY EVER DEAR SISTER:

"There will be an opportunity to send to Calcutta to-morrow, and I owe you a letter, and want to write it; but really I am so tired, I do not know how to begin, and I have no time. I am preparing a book for Burman mothers, a work their necessities have long demanded; but I feel incompetent to the task; especially, as there is no work in English suited to these poor dark-minded sisters. It must be written expressly for them, and modeled to suit their circumstances.

"But unfit as I am, it seems to have been

considered *my* duty, for I have been urged to it ever since I was at Maulmain. I have now a good assistant who happened accidentally to come here instead of going to Maulmain, but, as he is expecting every day to leave for Calcutta, I have to be busy day and night. I have scarcely leisure to eat or sleep. If I do sleep, I am lecturing to mothers. If I attend meeting, my thoughts are sermonizing instead of *listening* to sermons; if I read my Bible, (I look at no other book now,) the first thought is, what hint shall I get here for mothers. In fact, it is the all-absorbing subject. I am in too great haste to think of anything else. When I get tired out and feel 'down-hearted' about it, I think it will not be good for anything, and I shall have my labor and weariness to pay me for my trouble and anxiety. Well, you will say, if you cannot spare five minutes to write something more interesting than this, do not waste your paper. I really would like to interest you, but how? *The most interesting thing to me is, that I have got the Mothers' Book all prepared in English ex-*

cept one chapter, and half done in Burman; but stop, here is the old subject."

The book was finished, and, though its earnest Author has long since passed away from earth, it still lives, and is read by many a mother in that heathen land, who is guided by its counsels, cheered and encouraged, and instructed in the great duties of maternity, which hitherto were uncared for and unknown.

Her own character as a tender and affectionate mother, and her hallowed example, gave her peculiar opportunities for happily influencing those poor heathen females, who looked up to her as a pattern and guide. Through this channel she accomplished great good, the results of which are eternal. The very tenderness of Mrs. Comstock's own maternal feelings, and the judicious exercise of those faculties which pertain to a mother, gave her great power in this respect.

But though thus intensely anxious for the good of those around her, she had many a tender thought for the spiritual welfare of the beloved ones, whom she had left behind in highly favored America, as yet without a saving interest in heavenly things. Many a fervent prayer did she offer in their behalf at a Throne of Grace, and many a faithful appeal found its way to them across the wide ocean, for hers was a large and loving heart, which knew no narrow bounds in its generous ardor.

We quote an extract from a letter written by her to a beloved younger brother, urging upon his serious attention the claims of religion. After giving a description of the manners of the heathen, and their spiritual state, she concludes with the following earnest appeal.

"Thus far I have filled my sheet, yet have not said one word on that subject which most intimately concerns you, dear brother, and most deeply interests me in your behalf. You have never seen the debasing influence of heathenism, and you know not how great a debt of gratitude you owe—

> 'The goodness and the grace
> That on your birth have smiled.

Often as I look around me, and survey the mental waste, that on every side meets my view, I am constrained to offer thanksgiving and gratitude, that I, and my beloved brothers, and sisters were not born in heathen lands, where God was never known. Then I feel that I ought to labor with all my might to make my poor dark sisters of Arracan acquainted with the enlightening and life-giving power of the Gospel; but again, the thought returns, what if some of my dear friends with all their light and all their privileges should at last go down to death, eternal death! O! S——, it would be more tolerable for these heathen in that day than for you! I cannot tell you how anxious I feel lest you should grieve away the spirit of God; nor the anguish of the thought, that in eternity we *may* be more widely separated than even now. I try to pray the Father for you; yes, many times each day, does my voice ascend in supplications for my far-distant, beloved brothers; but I can do no more. If you would see God in peace, if you would dwell in heaven with God, Christ, and angels, your dear parents, brothers, and sisters, you must *repent now.* When you read this letter will you not resolve to improve the remainder of your life in preparation for death! May I not soon hear that my brother is resolved to live for God, heaven, happiness! I shall never see you more in time, dear S——, but may I not meet you a bright seraph in a world of bliss.

"Your very affectionate sister,

"S. D. COMSTOCK."

More than one reference has already been made in this volume to the tender and affectionate feelings of Mrs. Comstock as a *mother.* The following letters to her eldest daughter on her birth-days, of May 8, 1840, '41, and '42, will furnish, among many other acts, illustrations of her lively concern for the salvation of those who were so nearly committed to her care, and who never ceased to entwine around her heart.

"**Ramree, May 8, 1840.**

"TO LUCY ON HER BIRTH-DAY,—

"My dear little daughter, this is your birth-day. You are five years old. God, your Father in Heaven, has been very good to you. *He* has taken care of you five long years, and therefore you are now alive and well. Your papa and mama love you, and delight to supply your wants. But your Father in heaven will love you, if you are a good girl, a great deal better than papa and mama love you, and will take better care of you than they can do. God gave you your papa and mama, and your two dear little brothers. Therefore I hope you will love the good and kind God with all your heart; and that you will try to obey your parents, and love and be kind to your brothers. Never quarrel with them, but be always ready to please and assist them.

"Now you will not always do this, unless you get a new heart. For the heart you now have is very wicked, and makes you do wicked things. Then pray to God, my dear child, every day, for *a good, clean heart.* If you want to pray *right*, God will teach you. He loves to hear little children pray, and will listen to your prayers. Do not then, my dear child, let *one* day of this year pass, without praying that God will make you *a good girl.*

"Little Sophia Brown died when she was five years old, but she had a good heart. She loved Jesus Christ, and was happy when she died. She is now in heaven with that precious Saviour, who took little children up in his arms, and blessed them. Now if *you* are a good girl, God, your heavenly Father, will love you. Jesus Christ will love you, and your papa and mama will be very *very* happy Then, when you die, you will go and live in God's happy home, where all good children dwell.

"Now, my sweet girl, when you receive this letter, which your dear mama has written for your birth-day, go and pray to your Father in heaven, to make you his own dear child, and ask him to help you through this year to try to do those things only, which will please him.

"From your affectionate mama."

" ———, May 8, 1841.

"MY OWN DEAR LUCY,—

"This is your birth-day. You are six years old. God, your heavenly Father, has taken care of you ever since you were a tiny babe. He has watched over you when you were awake, and while you were asleep. He has kept you from all harm. He has healed you when you have been sick. He has given you food and clothes, a home and parents. He has taken care of your dear brothers. Yet, my dear daughter, you do not love this kind Father. You grieve him by your sins every day. You do not love the dear Saviour who died for Lucy. You know, my dear child, you have a soul that will never die; and unless you are sorry for your sins, and pray to God for a new heart, when your body dies, you will go out of it into that dreadful place where all wicked people live. You will not then be able to know more and more about the good God who made you. You will never be able to see the Saviour, and the good and happy people who live with him.

"I wish, Lucy, that you would, to-day, begin to pray to God for a new heart, to help you to love him, and obey your parents, and always do what is right. Think how many times you have sinned against God, and grieved the precious Saviour. Be sorry for your sins, and then *pray with all your heart.*

God will hear you, for he loves to hear little children pray. He has heard many little girls younger than you, and has given them new hearts. Try then, my dear Lucy, *this year*, to be a Christian, and have your name written in God's book of life.

"If you live till another birth-day, I hope it will find you a true disciple of Christ, then it will find you a happy child, loving and loved by all. You will not live with mama a great while, but if you are a Christian, I shall not feel so sad to part with you; because I shall hope to see you in heaven. Again, let me say, *pray for a new heart.*

"Your affectionate mother."

"————May 8, 1842.

"My dear Lucy—this day you are seven years old. God has watched over you by day and by night. When you have been sick, he has made you well; and he has brought you one year nearer to the grave, and to an *eternity* of happiness in heaven, or misery in hell.

"You are now, my dear Lucy, old enough to understand that you have a very wicked heart, that you must be sorry for your many sins, and believe in the precious Saviour, who alone can save you from the dreadful hell which your sins deserve. You know how great was the love of Jesus Christ for your *soul.* You know he came down from his happy home in heaven, and suffered and died in this wicked world. All this he did for *you,* my dear daughter, yes, for *you,* to save you from eternal burnings.

"And can you not, my dear child, love so kind, so gracious a Friend, one who has loved you *so much?* Can you not hate and forsake those dreadful sins, that make him suffer so much? Will you not begin, *to-day,* dear Lucy, to love and obey the dear Saviour? You cannot do it of yourself; but God will help you, if you pray to Him. He loves to listen to children's prayers. Ask Him to teach you how wicked your heart is; to help you to hate sin, and to love holiness; to teach you how to pray, so that He can hear and answer you; to help you to live so that He can love you as his own dear child.

"This is probably the last birth-day you will ever spend with your dear parents on earth; but, my dear Lucy, if you do as I have told you, God will be your Father and friend; and though we see you no more here, He will take care of you while you live, and when you die, will take you to his happy home above, where we shall hope to meet you again, and live with you, and love you for ever and ever. Strive then to be a Christian now; yes, *begin to-day*, to obey God in all things. This is the strongest wish of

"Your ever affectionate mother."

The tidings of a revival occurring in the vicinity of her native place, and of others in various parts of the country, gave Mrs. Comstock especial pleasure and interest in the prosperity of Zion; which she thus expresses to a correspondent.

"O," she exclaims, "I rejoice in the intelligence that revivals are multiplied around you—would that their delightful influence might reach and pervade this idol-trusting land! What a change, glorious change would one such revival effect here! My heart leaps at the thought, and shall it never be? Shall this valley never be vocal with the praise of its Creator? Shall these hills never echo the voice of universal prayer and praise to Him who so loved guilty Arracan, that He gave his own life's blood a sacrifice to ransom her from sin's enthralments? Yes! yes! it *must* be. God has promised it, and in that promise I often rest, when my heart would sink in view of the stupidity of some, and the hatred of others toward the *only* Saviour. I often tell the people, that though they despise and perish, others who come in their stead will be wiser and believe. 'Well,' they reply, 'if I lived in that time, I would believe too, but I cannot believe alone.'"

O how averse is human nature to the reception of Divine truth; how slow to believe; how tardy to repent. Long does the Saviour knock for admittance not only into hearts darkened and closed by superstition and falsities, but those, whose intellects are enlightened and cultivated, whose understandings are convinced, but who dare not come forward boldly alone, and acknowledge the entrance of the heavenly guest. How few of the great multitude of mankind are ready to receive that which gives life and liberty to the soul.

But though Mrs. Comstock was so intensely solicitous for the spiritual benefit of others, she did not neglect her own vineyard, and the cultivation of the Christian graces in her own soul. She desired to advance in piety and heavenly wisdom. It was a source of sorrow to her as it often is to the true Christian, that she made no greater progress in Divine things. She felt that she had a work to accomplish *within*, as well as without—a warfare to engage her watchful attention, and prayerful vigilance, against unseen and spiritual foes. Often in her letters she refers to the exercises of her own mind in this respect, lamenting her coldness, and ardently desiring the quickening influences of the Holy Spirit.

She in one of these remarks:

"I said I had cause to mourn and weep. Yes. I find cause for sorrow in the hard unrelenting heathen's state, and still greater cause do I find *in my own heart.* So little love to Christ, so little devotion to the service of God, so little melting of soul in view of the wretchedness of the heathen's eternity, so little penitence and humility in view of all my unfaithfulness! I have often said to myself, O could I know that I had been instrumental in saving *one soul*, it would be worth devoting a thousand lives to labor in a foreign clime far from kindred and friends!

"But I now feel, rather, that could I be *assured*, that I am what I *ought to be*, that I labor and feel and pray *as I ought*, that I was *accepted* of *God in all*, I could rest satisfied, though He should not see fit to honor the instrumentality of such a feeble worm, in the salvation of a soul. But, alas! I am too well aware, that in many things I offend, and *in all come short* of *duty*. Yet aside from all my deficiencies and all my sins, I believe I have had a good degree of enjoyment, of content and happiness, since I have been a stranger to my native land."

Again, after alluding to the faint prospect of meeting once more those whom she once fondly loved and still cherished, she remarks:

"This, however, is a privilege which we cannot expect on earth. And that I may enjoy it after this earthly pilgrimage is ended, I must strive daily for more of 'that mind which was in Christ Jesus.' How short, how uncertain a thing does life appear! To-day, we have heard that sister Jones of Bankok, has gone to her rest. Thus one after another of our little number is called home. How soon will you hear the same tidings of Sarah? It matters not how soon, if she has but the 'lamp trimmed and burning.' But I feel that I have lived thus far to but little, very little purpose.

"Once, when at Kyouk Phyoo, I seemed to be just passing death's open door. I thought, I felt, as I wish I could always now feel in reference to the perishing heathen. How infinitely trifling looked everything not connected with heaven and hell! The world and its vanities were less than nothing. How can we think so much of them when death is not staring us in the face? I think I have felt, for a week or ten days past, some desire to die to the world and its allurements, and to live as a candidate for the final retribution. But I am a mere dwarf in religion, real heart religion; and sometimes I fear I know nothing yet about it as I ought to know. Do you, dear parents, pray for us? Do you pray that we may abound in the love of God, and in usefulness among the heathen? You need not feel any anxiety about our temporal welfare; there is no danger in that respect. But keep the prayerful incense burning on the altar for our sakes."

Shortly after this, she wrote again in a similar spirit.

"I feel this climate to be very debilitating, and energy of mind decreases in as rapid a ratio as strength of body. But oh, if in my weakness Almighty strength is perfected in bringing some of these poor, deluded children of idolatry to Christ, it is all that I can desire. But I have too little love to God, too little compassion for these dying thousands, too little faith, too little of a spirit of prayer. Every thing here has a tendency to quench the fire of devotion—of true, heart-religion, and it is very hard to keep the flame alive. Sometimes I fear it is gone out

—wholly extinguished in my heart—so little warmth is imparted to religious duties.

"Though I sometimes feel sad, and perhaps a little discouraged, when I think how very, very little I have done since I came among the heathen, I know, and am persuaded, that my coming here was of God. He ordered and overruled most manifestly every thing in relation to it. And I do not, I have not, I never can, for an instant, regret that I left all dearest to my heart on earth. No; I only want to be more holy, that I may be more useful. I want to discharge my duty fully, faithfully, to these poor, weak children of superstition, and then leave the event, whether or not I am permitted to see them own Christ, in the hands of Him who ordereth all things after his own will. For this object will you not pray, often, and fervently pray? And then, when the duties, trials, and temptations of this probation are over, we shall reunite. Yes, though we meet no more in the flesh, we shall, methinks, reunite in the better land, where affection, filial, parental, and Christian, shall be strengthened, purified, perfected, and rendered eternal as the throne of God."

Though not exactly in its proper place, as to date, this seems a not unsuitable connection in which to place a valuable letter, addressed by Mrs. Comstock to a valued friend in Brookline. It will explain itself as the reader proceeds.

Ramree, July 8, 1840.

"MY DEAR FRIEND,—

"Your kind letter of October last, was received, with others in the box then sent, about the last of June. Your account about the last days of dear C——, interested me much. I was the more affected, as the tidings reached me when lying on a sick bed. A few days previous, the prospect seemed to be that it would prove my death-bed. My heavenly Father had again led me down to the brink of the grave; I looked into it with the expectation, that it would soon be my rest. The thought of death was at this time even more familiar than at the two former periods when I was brought low by the same dreadful disease. I had dwelt on it from day to day, and had in my mind selected the spot for my last resting place. Yet a wise God, whose thoughts are not as our thoughts, has seen fit again to raise me up. For what purpose? I cannot but often ask myself. I feel that I have yet done very little good. It may be that the Lord designs, by these repeated admonitions, *to prepare me* for doing some good. I would hope this may be the result. At all events, it is my desire and prayer, that this affliction may lead me to love God more, and to love the souls of the poor heathen more;—to seek for more holiness of heart, more entire consecration to the service of my Saviour;—and, in short, to '*hunger and thirst after righteousness;*' still unsatisfied till 'I awake in his likeness.'

"From the time that I first heard of our dear C.'s illness, and its probable termination, I have thought much on the dealings of God with us. You know we were intimate. Many a precious season of prayer have we enjoyed together in the little chapel at B———, for our loved Sunday-school classes. We used often to talk freely together of death. She had then the impression that consumption had commenced its work. Yet after her lungs were examined, she seemed encouraged. When I thought of coming to India, we thought I might be the *first* to 'go hence.' Yes, when I left, C. and H. were well; and I suppose my friends little thought, that *they* would be called first. Here I have been a good part of the last six years, the time of our separation, surrounded by sickness, disease, and death. To say nothing of slight attacks, I have *three times* been brought to death's door. Yet I still live, a monument of sparing mercy; while they, from a genial clime, surrounded by kind, affectionate friends, and every comfort of life, have been called to the presence of their Father, and our Father, of their God and our God.

"Yes, dear, *dear sisters!* they are now happy beyond the trials of time, in their heavenly home. How much wiser and holier are they now than we! Yet 'we a little longer wait.' C.'s death has come very near to me. It seems more like a dream than a reality. When I reflect on it, I cannot but wonder that I yet remain, 'a cumberer of the ground.' Truly God's ways are not as our ways. O, may I improve by these repeated admonitions, and be 'also ready.'

"I could weep with her dear, mourning, lonely husband. His heart must be deeply stricken. Yet I rejoice to hear that he is supported and comforted by the consolations of our holy religion. May he come forth from the furnace of repeated and heavy afflictions, 'as gold purified seven times!'

'How vain are all things here below,
How false, and yet how fair!'

"Still, the Christian is not left, under any circumstances, to sorrow as others who have no hope. We have a *Saviour*,—a faithful and ever present Friend,—a never-failing Source of joy;—yes, our best beloved Friend!

"You will be ready to ask what are our prospects of usefulness among these poor, wretched heathen. Would that I could tell you of a glorious work of grace among them, such as we hear of in our native land! But, alas, we still have to labor only *in hope*. There is little in the appearance of the natives to encourage us; but in the promises of God, there is much. Yes, we sometimes have a little faith to believe that we shall yet see converts multiplied here. 'He is faithful who hath promised.' There are one or two Mussulmen who encourage us to hope, that they will before long come out openly for Christ. Yet the very best of them are so ignorant, so fickle-minded, that we feel we cannot trust much in appearances, however pleasing.

"Could you have witnessed the great, old stone idol, just opposite our house, as it was when we came here, four or five months ago, and then have seen the transactions of the day before yesterday, you would have concluded, that there had been *a revival of idolatry.* Four months since it stood, a huge, hideous, soul-destroyer, nakedly exposed to the scorching sun by day, and the heavy dews by night. The roof and walls which once protected it were gone; the last vestige of them had fallen, leaving the bare posts standing. It was seldom visited. I recollect seeing it worshiped only in one or two instances; and those were during the great feast of the new year, when no deity, however obscure, is neglected. Early one morning, two women, accompanied by two little girls, came with plates of rice and bunches of flowers, and prostrated themselves before the dumb image. During ten or fifteen minutes, they were engaged in 'vain repetitions,' with their uplifted hands, and heads bowed to the earth. After 'shecosing' several times, quite down to the earth, they rose and presented their offerings. The dear little children followed their mothers' example. It really made me weep to see *how ready* those little infants were with tiny uplifted hands, and bended knees, to do reverence to a senseless block of stone. O! thought I, when will they learn thus early to do nobler homage to Him who said, 'Suffer the little children to come unto me!' There too, I learned a lesson of *maternal duty*, from those devotees of heathenism.

"But to return to the old image, as he now is,—no longer left desolate and alone, An old, silver-headed man, a devoted child of idolatry, has erected a fine new house over him, to shield his already time-and-tempest-worn head from the pouring torrents of rain. The day before yesterday, in the morning, while it was yet early, a procession of people, preceded by music, priests, and offerings, marched slowly along to pay their morning devotions. The grand object of the parade was to array his godship in a fine, new, yellow 'pu sue,' splendidly decorated with tassels and gold leaf. Their devotions were long and solemn, and surely no Christian could listen to the deep-toned, serious response of the deluded multitude, without a feeling of solemnity and pity. The author of so pious and sacred an offering, could not fail, in the eyes of the people, to secure to himself a great share of merit. Doubtless his gratified ears were often that day saluted with 'That du, that du.' [Well done, well done.] Yes, that sixth of July was a memorable day for the old, dumb image of De lun Kaing. He no longer remains destitute, forsaken, and naked; but sits arrayed in his new, glittering garb, with horrible and silent dignity, to receive the daily offerings of wilfully blinded zeal.

O! my heart bleeds to think of the eternity that is before these poor, wretched souls. They madly reject the offers of salvation, revile the precious and only Saviour, and sink down to endless burnings. Well might we say of thee, 'O Arracan, Arracan, how often would I have gathered thy children together, but ye would not!'"

CHAPTER VIII.

Progress of the Mission—Reinforcement—Persecution of the Karens—Religious interest at Ramree—Encouragement to labor.

> **They scattered the seed in faith and hope,**
> **They scattered it far and wide;**
> **And some sprang forth to eternal life,**
> **And some to appearance died.**

THE progress of the Mission at Ramree, during the years of Mr. and Mrs. Comstock's labor, was comparatively slow. The truths of the Gospel had made an impression upon the minds of the people, but as yet they were too timid to come boldly forward and acknowledge the fact. To human appearance, the good seed sown fell upon hard and stubborn hearts, and darkened understandings; but here and there, like a gleam of heavenly light, was a token of the illuminating power of the Gospel.

In other sections of the province the work

was prosecuted with more apparent success. Among the Karen part of the population, many interesting cases of conversion occurred, and serious attention to the claims of the new religion.

In 1840, the Missionaries were cheered and reinforced by the arrival of Rev. Eugenio Kincaid and wife, who came to take charge of the interest at Akyab, having previously been engaged in the work at Maulmain and Ava. Rev. Mr. Abbott and his wife were also appointed to the Mission at Sandoway. Mrs. Comstock, Mrs. Kincaid, and Mrs. Stilson each conducted a school for native boys and girls, with a fair prospect of success.

At that time, Burmah Proper was closed to Missionary efforts, in consequence of difficulties existing between the Burman and English governments. Much opposition was manifested on the part of the authorities to Missionary influence. Several stations were of necessity relinquished for a season, and left in charge of native assistants.

This was a source of great regret to the Missionaries; they trembled, and not without reason, for the fate of their little churches, left, as it were, like sheep in the midst of wolves, exposed to temptation and persecution; and they feared much lest the timid faith of the newly-made communicants should fail before the sword of persecution, and the worldly loss sure to be experienced by all in a greater or less degree, who should hold fast to the doctrine they had embraced.

Often and earnestly did the prayers of the "teachers" ascend to Him whose grace is sufficient for all things, that He would keep as in the hollow of His hand, all those precious ones who had been called by His name, and whose hearts had been turned from their dark idolatry to the worship of the true and living God.

The poor Karens, whose simple, open hearts had been most willing to receive the Gospel, and yield to Divine influences, suffered most for their attachment to the truth, and in 1843 were persecuted by the Burman government, with great cruelty.

They had constructed at Baumee a chapel for religious exercises, under the superintendence of Shway Bay, a native assistant. A report was circulated by those opposed to

Christianity, that this chapel was to be a palace for a Karen general, who would shortly invade Burmah at the head of a large army, in the meanwhile, making it his head quarters. It was said the palace was large and strong, with one hundred and fifty posts, and what was more ominous than all, was surmounted with a royal cupola, which in Burmah is never allowed to be built only on the palaces of the kings, or on religious edifices. Whether this report was credited or not by the Burmese authorities, it served as an occasion for manifesting great hostility to the Karen Christians in the various villages, who were closely watched and treated with unrelenting severity.

On one occasion a number of them came over to the Baumee chapel to meet the Rev. Mr. Abbott, who was to be there and preach, and administer the ordinance of baptism.

After a very interesting and delightful service, in the course of which Mr. Abbott baptized 150 converts and ordained two pastors, the Karens who had come over from Burmah commenced their return home. But on the way, they were seized by the

Burman guards, and cruelly tortured, whipped, and carried in chains to that terrible place, a Burmese prison, there to await, amid more suffering, the decision of the Burman king. Terror of course, spread through the jungles; some apostatized, some denied that they had ever worshiped the true God, while others stood firm and unyielding as the eternal hills which surrounded them. None of the prisoners (about thirty, besides the little children who followed their mothers to prison) wavered at all, though most unmercifully tortured to make them renounce their religion. It was feared eventually, that some would be tortured to death, and that more would be induced through pain and fear to deny the Lord that bought them.

"Only think," wrote Mrs. Comstock in view of this persecution, "you who can sit in the sanctuary of the Lord surrounded with multitudes of like precious faith with yourselves, and permitted to listen without fear to the preaching of the truth—only think of those poor dear Karens, hunted like partridges on the mountains, cast into prison, loaded with chains, whipped, and tortured with all that cruelty which a Burmese well knows how to exercise, and all on account of their love to Jesus. Think of feeble women chained two and two, with young infants at their breasts, and then raise a prayer of faith for those suffering ones, who purchase their liberty to worship the God of their salvation with their blood. Pray that they may have grace to endure to the end, and glorify God in all.

"The Burman officers," she continues, "know not what to make of the Karen Christians; they say they are, 'tai-ket'—[very hard,] the more they beat them the firmer they are in refusing to recant. What the result of all this persecution will be, 'He who sitteth in the heavens' alone can tell."

In these unfortunate people, Mrs. Comstock felt a deep interest. Yet she felt none the less, though of a different kind, for those among whom she was laboring, who were less willing to receive the word of Life, while needing it equally with the poor Karens. The more indifferent they were, the more she redoubled her efforts among them to win them to salvation and God. She was willing to toil on in faith and hope, though the day of her harvest was appointed for another world than this.

But though the Missionaries were often cast down, they were not deterred from unwearied efforts. With regard to their location in this place, Mr. C—— remarks in 1840:

"We were never before so favorably situated for Missionary work, as we are now. Our new house proves to be most favorably located. The road which passes just in front of it is the great thoroughfare to and from the numerous villages in the interior, and hundreds travel it almost daily. We have a spacious verandah in front where the people can sit and rest, and listen to the glad tidings of great joy. On some days, a hundred or more call upon us, on other days few, but on the whole our facilities for spreading among the people a knowledge of the truth are very great. Many who call listen to the truth a few minutes, take a tract, and go away never to return. Some come two or three times, and a few repeatedly. These heathen are very dark-minded, and it is difficult to make them understand the simplest truths of the word of God. They are, too, very hard-hearted, and it is far more difficult to make them *feel* than *understand.* They seem to have no moral sense. I fear I am greatly deficient in faith; the unbelieving inquiry, 'Can these dry bones live?' often arises in my mind, while I am engaged in preaching Christ to a crowd of darkened, stupid idolaters. That 'nothing is too hard for God' is support and encouragement enough to us, when we can really feel it.

"We are trying now to see what can be done in the way of schools. Several scholars are promised, but I fear we shall not have many to begin with. A few Mussulmen seem to be considerably interested in the Christian religion; but I do not know that there are now any decidedly encouraging inquirers here. There seems to be quite a general disposition with those Mugs who have heard a good deal of the truth to say, 'It's all very good; you believe just as we do, only we call the same things by different names.'"

But as time wore on, they received more frequently the blessed assurance that their labor was not in vain. They were also cheered and encouraged by the evident success which attended Mr. Comstock's itinerant labors in various sections of the country. On one occasion while absent upon a tour, preaching, distributing tracts, and teaching, he wrote home to Mrs. C——, such joyful tidings of the interest manifested, that she thus expressed her grateful emotions in a letter to her sister.

"Let us take courage; the signs of the times denote good things in store for Arracan. The day of her redemption must be at hand, but there is much work, *hard work* to be done, ere the land will be possessed. And where are the laborers? These valleys and hills with their thousands and hundreds of thousands of precious but dying souls, and their hosts of soul-destroying idols, echo, *where?* Think for one moment of two or three feeble, fainting Missionaries for nearly three hundred thousand souls, and part of these devoted, in a great measure, to the preparation of needful books, and the press, at which work their services are invaluable. O where is the Spirit of Christ! Has it deserted the churches of our native land? Are there none among the multitudes of their members, whose hearts yearn over these poor deluded ones, who are fast going down to people the dark regions of despair, untaught of One mighty to save? Is there *not one* to respond to the cry, which comes up long and loud from every town, and village, and hamlet of this vast province 'Come over and help us.' Can the church stand acquitted of the blood of souls at the last great day, if she turn a deaf ear to that cry? If I had a voice that could reach the hearts of the 'young men and maidens' of our happy land who are full of faith and the Holy Ghost, *I would plead with them, by all that is desirable in heaven, by all that is fearful in perdition, by all that is efficacious in the blood of the cross for the redemption of souls, to come to the rescue of Arracan, to come and reap its whitened fields.*

"The 'seed of the kingdom' which has

so long been sown, is just ready to spring up, and it will yet, I trust, yield a rich harvest to the glory of God."

Shall such a stirring appeal have been made in vain by her whose tongue is now motionless in death?

CHAPTER IX.

Full confirmation in the path of duty—Letter to her step-father—Retrospection—Continued and deep interest—A grateful heart.

Whatsoe'er of ill befall me,
Be my journey short or long,
Here am I, for thou didst call me,
In *this* faith my soul is strong.

THERE was one pleasing consciousness which Mrs. Comstock possessed as the months and years of her Missionary career rolled on, which cheered her in her labors, and strengthened her in the discharge of her responsible duties. It was that she had not erred in judgment, or mistaken the path of duty, when she embarked in Missionary enterprise. Never, amid severe toil and suffering, did she repent having engaged in the sacred work, or have a single doubt of her being heaven-directed. In a letter to an intimate friend, written after she had been four years in Arracan, she wrote:

"Never, *no, never, for a moment* from the time that the Board said to me 'you may go' until now, have I felt even the shadow of a 'secret misgiving' as to the path of duty. I believe, fully and unequivocally, that unworthy, unfit, and unfaithful as I am, I am where *God* has led me, and where *He would have me labor.* I am as happy, as contented, yea, and more so, as with so little love to God, I could be in any spot from the rising to the setting sun. If I cannot do good here, it will not be from lack of opportunity; I surely could not in any other place. Time is short, what we do must be done quickly, and, if I should forsake these heathen, to spend my remnant of days among the 'loved and lovely' at home, I should feel that in so doing, I was seeking *my own pleasure,* rather than to do my heavenly Father's will. This thought alone would render the dying hour one of bitterness and remorse."

And again after the lapse of a few more years, she wrote:

"I do not regret the events of this day eight years. But how little have I done? I have been a most unprofitable servant, less than the least, and unworthy the important trust committed to me. But unworthy as I am, and unprofitable as my life has been, I cannot think I erred in coming here. I am guilty of having so little faith, love, and holi ness, but I am here, because God hath sent me hither. I cannot regret it. No! whatever may befall me, whatever may befall my children after me, I have the consolation of knowing that God chose my inheritance for me, and He cannot err. He said by His providence, and in language too plain to be misunderstood or doubted, 'Go;' and I came in obedience to His mandate only."

In the same strain also she wrote her step-father, of which the following is an extract:

"The Sabbath sun is just going down in the west. I have a moment merely, before the evening prayer-meeting, and that I will spend in conversing with you. I have been thinking a good deal of father this afternoon, and of your sermons, and comments on passages of Scripture, which I have so often listened to with pleasure. Sometimes the thought that I shall never more on earth behold your venerable countenance, nor listen to the voice of parental admonition, causes a moment's *sadness*, but *no regret.* No, though aware that when I left you, I lost a father's care, a father's counsel, and a father's home, yet conscience tells me, that in so doing, I performed a duty that I owed myself, the heathen, and my God. And I *cannot* REGRET it. I shall never more meet my dear father in the flesh; I shall no more sit beside him, and talk of earthly or of heavenly things. But shall I not see him face to face in glory? Shall I not be permitted there to join him in the song 'Worthy the Lamb?' And beside us shall not the voices of redeemed Arracanese sweetly echo the song? Yes,

'There on a green and flowery mount
Our weary souls shall sit,
And with transporting joy recount
The labors of our feet.'

"'Will not that, dear father, be a happy day? We shall there feel no loss of spiritual privileges—no more temptation—no more sin. And to dwell with Jesus will be the consummation of bliss. More than this, we know that our joys are eternal."

On the seventh anniversary of her Missionary life, Mrs. Comstock indulged in the following personal reflections:

"*July* 1, 1841.—This night, seven years ago, was the last I passed, or ever expect to pass, under our dear father's roof. It was the Sabbath night after the consecration of the Missionaries at Baldwin Place Church. Yes, *seven* years have fled, and borne their account upward, a solemn, irreversible account.

"We are yet, through Sovereign Grace, alive, and permitted to labor for lost heathen souls. This is a privilege which I do not deserve, and which I do not know how to prize as I ought. May the Lord enable me to realize more and more the *worth* of the *soul*, and enable me also to put forth efforts commensurate therewith. There is nothing in this world, else, worth living for. Nothing but to try to do some good to *souls*, and something to advance the cause of Him who died for us. How trifling will the world, and its best, brightest joys, look to us from the banks of the river of death!—Yet how do our hearts cling to these transient pleasures.' How little, very little *real* love to God is to be found in our hearts, if we carefully analyze our feelings, motives, and designs. I often feel that much love dwells not in my heart, as an active, operating principle. When I left my native land, I did not imagine that the close of seven years of Missionary life would find me such a *skeleton* of a Christian, with scarcely a breath of spiritual life: especially after having been made the recipient of multiplied mercy and goodness."

It was once suggested to Mr. Comstock by a friend, that he should return to his native land and labor, as he saw so little *visible* fruit from his toils in a foreign field. In reply to this Mrs. Comstock remarks:

"We trust the seed we are now sowing, sometimes in hope, and sometimes with a faint heart, will spring up and yield a glorious harvest. It would be pleasant, it would cheer our hearts, to see converts multiplied, but it should be our chief concern to do *our* part faithfully, and then be willing to leave the event in God's hands.

"Brother O——, in a letter yesterday received, urges it as a reason why Mr. C—— should return home, that he sees so little fruit after laboring so long. 'What would you think, were the indications of Providence,' he asks, 'if you had labored so long in your native land, with no more success?' But now it seems to me, the reason he urges for a return, should induce us to remain and labor so much the more. He is mistaken if he thinks the labors of eight years are for nought. No, they will bear an important part in the great work of Arracan's conversion to Christ. The fallow ground is being broken up, and prepared for the seed which is to yield an abundant harvest. Light is spreading; by *many*, very *many*, the truth is acknowledged; *fear* keeps them back from a *public* profession of it, or rather their *hearts* are not filled with the Spirit; the *understanding* only is enlightened. The name of Christ and the true religion is *known*, or *has been heard* almost through the length and breadth of the land but alas! it finds a dwelling in no heart as yet. We should faint were it not for the promises of God's word, which stand pledged for the redemption of Arracan.—In view of its great destitution shall we, who profess to have our treasures laid up in heaven, shrink from the work, and leave these precious souls to go down to spiritual darkness for ever and ever, without having once heard of Him who is mighty to save? No; when I view the subject in this light, I am ashamed that I do so little, feel so little, pray so little. I could wish I had as many bodies as the fabled Hydra had heads; one should be placed here; another at Kyouk Phyoo; and a third among the Kyens. Only think of the vast multitudes of that interesting race, who inhabit the fastnesses of the mountains, without a written language, without religion, without a God! Yet they have no one to guide their dark minds, and point them upward to Him who created them. They are a sister tribe of the Karens; and who knows but the same efforts among them would be attended with similar results as among the latter tribe? There is every reason to believe they would. Oh! if the multitudes of Christians in America, who never yet made a *sacrifice*, could but see with their own eyes the situation of this vast province, methinks their hearts and their purses would be open, and they would say to their sons, and their daughters, 'Go, speak to that people, the words of life; go, and the Lord be with thee.'"

Amidst the arduous labors of Mrs. Comstock, and her unwearied zeal, it is interesting to notice the gratitude with which she received sympathy and kind attention from her friends in America, and the effect such manifestations had upon her mind. A Missionary, though he has forsaken father and mother, brothers, sisters, and friends for the Saviour's sake, is still connected with such in the spirit. He is human still, and as such feels an interest in the scenes and loved faces he shall never witness again on earth. Some minds prize the joys they can taste no more except in memory, by the measure of their deprivations. On such, tokens of sympathy, delicate attentions to manifold wants, words of encou ragement and affection, a friendly letter costing but little effort on the part of the writer; or gifts that comfort the weary body, and thereby refresh the soul, fall like heavenly manna and thrill the heart with delight.

Much has been done by the church in this respect for the isolated brethren and sisters in foreign lands; but, without sacrifice, there might be much more. In our worldliness and ease, we are apt to forget those who labor and suffer for the interests of Zion. Oftener, and without the shadow of a sacrifice, might the friendly message, and the token of affectionate remembrance find their way over the wide ocean to those who in poverty and loneliness preach the glad tidings of salvation. We can do more than pray for them, though the prayer of faith avails much. Are there not duties which God requires at our hands, the neglect of which will bring to our ears the language in the last great day, "Inasmuch as ye did it not to the least of one of these, ye did it not to me."

Mrs. Comstock, on one occasion, after the receipt of some articles which she had much desired, says:

"How kind to send me so many useful things! Can I ever repay my dear friends? Yes, I'll try to be more holy, more devoted, more assiduous and self-denying in endeavoring to lead these poor heathen to Jesus. I'll try to pray more for and with them; try, in short, to be more useful; and that will be the return you will ask, I know. Such resolutions are called forth by every packet from my dear friends at home. I read your letters—my heart is melted by proofs of affection, and sympathy, and interest in the heathen; and then I think, now I will try to be better, more useful, and more deserving your sympathy and love.

"*I think each letter from my dear American relatives and friends makes me love them more, love the heathen more, love Christ more*, and incites new emotions of gratitude. But oh, how little do I feel compared with what I should feel; my heart is cold and callous. O, for a new life in Christ Jesus!"

CHAPTER X.

A Missionary mother's sacrifice—Views and feelings on the occasion—Decision—Sustaining grace—The parting scene —Letters from Mr. and Mrs. Comstock to their children.

> O tell me if there any is
> In strength and depth surpassing this,
> The love a mother feels—
> Behold the heart by faith allied
> To Him who for its ransom died
> A mightier love reveals!

AMONG the many sacrifices to be made in her Missionary career, of which Mrs. Comstock had counted the cost in the outset, there was one which she overlooked; nor could it be estimated, for the feelings which composed the sacrifice had not then been awakened in her bosom.

But as years rolled by, and one jewel after another was entrusted to her keeping, and her heart throbbed with maternal love and solicitude, then the shadow of it darkened her soul. It stole in upon her joy at morning, at noon, and at even, when she performed the tender offices of affection, when she hushed her little ones to sleep with the sweet songs of infancy, or listened to their childish prattle; but most of all, as she saw them grow in strength and years. Her watchful eyes had long since shown her that her Burman home would be no fitting place for the judicious training of her beloved children, and that ere long they must be removed far from her and those heathen regions, to receive that physical and intellectual culture, and pure spiritual influence necessary to their well-being and highest good. Justice and prudence both forbade the attempt—to rear them in a land destitute of mental and religious privileges, and filled with vice and unholy examples, which would not fail to affect for evil more or less, the young minds exposed to their daily and almost hourly contact. Yes, they must be given up; the care which a mother feels, and so loves to feel, must be transferred to other hands, and fill other hearts than hers.

She had given up home, parents, brothers

sisters, and friends, but yet a greater sacrifice remained to be made, equally a part of the cost, and the only one upon which she had not counted well. Her children, nearer and dearer than any of these, must be relinquished for the sake of that cause to which she had devoted herself—the redemption of the heathen. But the prospect of this was overwhelming, and the hearts of both parents were wrung with anguish at the idea of a separation. Nor was the decision necessary to its accomplishment performed without a severe struggle between the voice of duty, and the pleadings of parental affection.

Often did they bow before a throne of grace, and plead for strength in this hour of trial, to obey the voice which in their ears, sounded like the voice of God to Abraham, when he bade him offer as a sacrifice his son, the child of promise, of hope and love. Mrs. Comstock's own personal feelings on this trying occasion were thus expressed in a communication to a friend.

"Our children" she remarks, (by way of apology for writing so freely of them,) "are but another name for self. You are right in supposing that I have many anxious thoughts about their future lot; *how many* and *how anxious* no human being can ever know. I am not decided as to whether it is best to send them from me, or rather from this country. From experience and observation, my own as well as that of others, I am convinced that our children cannot be properly educated and fitted for the greatest usefulness in this country; that I shall wrong my children, *seriously wrong* them, by suffering them to grow up, inhaling, day after day, and year after year, the fatal miasma with which the whole moral atmosphere of this country is so fearfully impregnated. On this point my *judgment* has long been convinced. Shall we, then, go home with our children, and see them educated under the genial influence of a Christian sky. Or shall we send them away, and commit their best interests, for time and for eternity, to stranger hands, who do not, *cannot* feel a *mother's responsibility,* however much and conscientiously they may strive to perform a mother's duties?

"As a general rule, I believe a mother's

duty to her children is second only to her duty to her Creator. How far Missionary mothers may be exempt from this rule, it is difficult to decide. A mother who has spent eight, ten, or twelve of her best years among the heathen, may be expected to be well acquainted with their language, manners, customs, and habits of thought and feeling. She has *proved* herself their friend, and gained their confidence and affection. She is, as it were, just prepared for extensive usefulness. At this period, shall she go and leave them, with none to tell them of Him who came to ransom their souls from sin and its penalty? Or, if another is raised up to fill her place, it must be years—years during which many precious immortals must go down to a dark, a fearful eternity, ere she is prepared to labor efficiently among them.

"I see no other way than for each individual mother prayerfully to consider the subject, and let her own conscience decide as to her duty. As to my own private feelings on this subject, after long, serious, and prayerful consideration, I have come to the conclusion that it is best to send our eldest two to America in the course of another year, should a good opportunity offer. This decision, be assured, has not been gained without many tearful conflicts with maternal affection. You are right when you judge this to be the greatest cross the Missionary is called to bear. When we left forever the land of our birth, the home, sweet home of our sunny childhood, and all those beloved friends and relatives, who were dearer to us than life, many thought we were making a great sacrifice. So it was. And deep and sincere seemed the sympathy that was evinced on our account. Yet the pangs of that separation are not to be compared with those which must rend that mother's heart who feels compelled to send from her fond embrace, those precious little ones to whom she has been the means of giving life—almost in the infancy of their existence, too, with no fixed principles and habits, and without a hope of ever seeing them again in time. This, surely forms the climax of a Missionary's sacrifices. But if God, the kind Author of all our blessings, require even this, shall we say, It is too much? Shall we withhold even Isaac? No; may we rather strive to commit ourselves and our precious offspring in faith to His care, who has said, 'Leave thy fatherless children to me.' They are, in one sense, *orphans.* But if rendered so by what we feel to be obedience to our Heavenly Father's will, will He not be to them a father and protector? Will He not more than supply the place of the most affectionate earthly parents?"

At another time she wrote:

"Notwithstanding the trial before me, which far surpasses every other I have even *thought* of, unless it be Mr. C.'s death, I do not regret the events of this day eight years since. No; as I then gave up all my dear earthly relatives and friends, at His command who said 'Lo, I am with you alway,' so now, I look to Him alone to sustain me in another and severer trial, which is equally of *His* own direction. Yes, here is all my trust and refuge. If it were not for the consciousness of *doing right*, of being in *the path of duty*, I could not, no, I *could not* sustain it. As it is, I expect my faith will sometimes grow weak, and well nigh fail, perhaps—but—I must look upward; I dare not look to any earthly source. I *cannot* lean on an arm of flesh. I know it *would not*, *could not* sustain me; but enough—why write I thus? You do not, cannot understand my feelings, nor can any but a Missionary mother. Pray for me; pray for those dear children who are so soon to be orphans, at an age, too, when they most need the watchful care of parental affection. This thought is at times almost too much for my aching, bursting heart to endure. Had not my Saviour, yes, and a compassionate Saviour, added these two words, 'and children,' to the list of sacrifices for his sake, I might think it more than was required."

Such were the emotions with which this truly devoted mother contemplated the trial she was soon called to endure.

Could any one, in view of such noble sentiments and strong convictions of duty, make accusation against a heart that thus felt and suffered, as possessing little or no natural feeling? Yet this was the conclusion drawn in many instances when children born of American parents were first sent home from

India to be educated. It was said the Missionaries were wanting in those feelings of parental affection which God has implanted in the human breast, in being thus willing to relinquish the care of their offspring. Christians, even, uttered words of reproach—that the Missionaries could thus act, when to *them* it was like plucking out the right eye, and crucifying the dearest desires of the heart. In Mrs. Comstock's own language it was "the climax of a Missionary's sacrifices." It was not from a *want* of love, but from its excess, that they thus acted, had there been no other motives compelling them to make the sacrifice. Whilst a blind affection, selfish in its promptings, would have retained them in a heathen land, the same love, purified by religion and ennobled by reason, sent the dear objects of parental solicitude, to find a home among strangers, but God's own favored people. But this was not their prevailing motive in the discharge of so painful a duty. The cause they had espoused with every energy, spiritual and bodily, demanded the sacrifice, and there was enough of suffering connected with it, without the sting of a consciousness that by some their motives would be misinterpreted and their conduct censured.

The feelings of Mrs. Comstock were noble as well as just, and in perfect harmony with the resolute devotion which formed so large an element in her character. When her judgment had brought her to the conclusion that she *ought* to part with her children, both for their sake and the sake of the heathen, then her decision was made to have them go, though, as she herself says, not without a severe struggle with affection.

Now she commenced preparations for their departure. With a throbbing heart but firm hand, she gathered together their little articles of clothing, touching them with fingers of love for the last time she felt upon earth. It was pain for her to know that all those offices of affection, and ministrations to the many little wants, which childhood requires, would henceforth be rendered by stranger hands. It was pain for her to feel, as she wrote to the friends of her youth, to receive her orphaned ones under their roof, and to their fireside; that *there her* feet could never follow, and *her* only chance of meeting them was in—heaven.

But amidst sorrow like this, and prayers and tears, the work of preparation went steadily on. A brother Missionary—the Rev. Eugenio Kincaid with his wife, was about returning for a period to America, and it was resolved the children should accompany them.

The hour of parting came; she clasped her arms around them, and gave them the last, the farewell kiss, with that intensity of emotion which only a mother's heart can feel. Nature plead mightily in these moments of conflict, but grace triumphed, and she exclaimed, amid her tears and anguish, "O, Jesus, I do this for thee!"

Saying these words, she resigned them to the arms of her husband, who led them on board the ship which was to convey them to America. And while, with faltering steps, and vision dimmed with fast-falling tears, she turned to her partly desolated home, the bark with its precious freight sailed from that heathen shore, bearing a mother's precious jewels away forever.*

Does the reader desire any additional evidences of this mother's love? They are at hand. While those dear objects of affection were yet in Calcutta, she thus addresses them.

* Of this affecting scene Mr. Kincaid gives the following account: which we are permitted to copy from his own autograph in the Album of a friend.

"It was nearly dark when brother and sister Comstock were informed that we must be on board ship that night. It was a trying moment. Mrs. Comstock, taking her two children by the hand, walked with us a few yards. Here, gazing upon their upturned faces for a little time, she impressed upon their cheeks a mother's last kiss, and turning around, raised her hands, uttering in broken accents, 'This I do for Christ! this I do for the heathen!'

"Brother Comstock went on board ship with us, and remained till about nine in the evening. But he must leave. Again and again he folded his Lucy and Oliver in his arms, gave them a father's last blessing, bathing their faces with his tears. His whole frame trembled with emotion. He went down the side of the ship, and as the little boat was gliding off in the dark, he looked up, and I heard—they were the last words I ever heard from that lamented Missionary—'Brother Kincaid remember—*six men for Arracan.*'

"In a few months his wife and his two youngest children lay side by side, in a grave overshadowed by an aged tamarind. In less than one year more he followed his dear wife and two lovely babes; and so they *all* sleep on the shores of Arracan." [J. N. B.

"Ramree, Oct. 16, 1842.

"MY DEAR, VERY DEAR CHILDREN,

"Though you are far, very far away, mama has thought a great deal about you to-day. We got home yesterday morning, and found the house, the goats, the ducks, and flowers all here. Ko Kulah and Ko Baing were here too, but no Lucy and Olly. [Oliver.]

"I went into your room, and there was Lucy's bed, and Olly's bed, but no Lucy or Olly to sleep in them. This is God's holy Sabbath day, and when we had worship this morning, I looked all around for Lucy and Olly to come and read and pray with us. Then at breakfast, I wanted to give you some coffee, but your chairs stood empty. At worship, when papa preached, I wanted to find you as usual, but no Lucy or Olly were here. Since dinner, I have no Lucy or Olly to read and talk with. I cannot hear you say the Commandments as I used to do, on Sabbath evening. I miss your Sabbath lessons too, in the Testament and hymn-book. But my dear children, you will read and learn your little verses in your Testament and hymn-book, I hope, to say to Nilly's mama and Jane. I hope you will be very good and quiet on God's holy Sabbath, and not play at all. Always obey them very quickly and willingly in all they say to you. Try to make them as little trouble as possible. For they are very kind to let you go to America with them, and to take care of you on the way. Be very kind to Nilly, Totty, and baby; love them, and try to take care of baby. Never quarrel, or speak cross to them, but play prettily together, and please each other.

"Especially, my dear Lucy and Olly, remember to pray to God every day. Pray for a new heart, and remember that God sees you all day and all night long. Do nothing that you are afraid to have God see you do. Pray for your dear papa, and mama, and Robert, who love you so much. We all think and talk of you a great deal; and though we love to have you to live with us, and feel very sad that we cannot see you here again; yet we are glad that you are going where you can learn a great many things that you could not learn here. Your grandpa and grandma will love you too very much, and will be very kind to you. I hope you will become Christians, and will love these poor heathen enough to come out here again, when you are grown big, and tell them about Christ.

"A good many natives have come here since we got home, to ask about you both. They say they remember you very much."

"Monday morning.

"MY DEAR, VERY DEAR CHILDREN,—

"I must send this letter to the post-office to-day, and can only write a little more. One thing more mama wishes you both to remember;—that is, for Lucy and Olly always to love one another very much, and *never speak or look cross to each other.* Now, my precious children, remember this, for you are far away from papa, and mama, and Robert, and must therefore love one another the more. We shall always love you very, very much, and shall be *so* happy to hear from you both often. It will make mama's sad heart happy to hear you are both good children. Robert talks a great deal about Lucy and Olly, and wants to see you very much. He says he '*will go and see you.*' I asked him just now what he would have me write to his dear brother and sister? He said, 'say good morning, Lucy, Olly.' He says he loves you '*both arms full.*' Yesterday he found a great spider on a great round bunch of its eggs, and he remembered how *you* used to like to see them, so he said he 'would catch it, and tie it up, and send it to Lucy and Olly;' but I think he forgot it when he had done bathing. It was in your bathing room. Take good care of your clothes, and try to be neat and clean always. Write to your dear papa and mama often, as soon as you can write a letter. I wish you would learn to write soon.

"Lucy, when you read this, please give Olly a sweet kiss on each cheek, and tell him mama sent them. Olly, will you please to give Lucy the same, and tell her they came from mama. Now, be dear good children, and think how happy you will thus make papa and mama. Accept this, with the deep love of your ever affectionate mama."

Would it not be an act of injustice were we here to withhold an expression of a father's love to his children? There lies before us a letter from Mr. Comstock to these dear children, which he wished to be delivered to them on the voyage, on New Year's Day. It thus reads:—

"Ramree, Jan. 1, 1843.

"MY DEAR LUCY AND OLLY:

"A very happy New Year to you, is the sincere wish of your papa and mama. This year is called 1843, because it is eigh teen hundred and forty-three years since our Lord Jesus Christ came into this world, to die for sinners. How good he was to die on the cross, that we might not go to hell! He is the only Saviour, and no one who does not love him can go to heaven. Do you, my dear children, love that precious Saviour? Do you believe in him, and pray to him every day, to take away your sins, and save your souls? The poor heathen, who worship idols, have no Saviour, but you know that Jesus can save, and will save those who love him.

"Will you not, my dear Lucy and Olly, now, on this first day of a new year, begin to love the Saviour, and try to do what he wishes you to do? If you do, then this will indeed be a happy new year to you; and your papa and mama will be happy too, when they hear that you have become Christians. Pray for your little brother Robert, that he also may become a Christian while young. God has said, 'They that seek me early, shall find me.'

"I suppose that you will receive this letter, when you are far off on the sea, and you will know that papa did not write it on January 1, 1843. This letter tells you what papa and mama would like to say to you on New Year's Day, and so I dated it as if it was written then. It is Nov. 2, 1842.

"Now while I am writing this, I do not know whether we shall be alive on the next New Year's Day, or whether both of you will be alive then; I hope, however, that we may all live much longer, and be good, and do good. Then we shall be sure to live together, a happy family in heaven. Robert too, I think, will want to wish you a happy new year, and give each of you two good kisses, which you may ask Jane to give you for him; also please ask her to kiss you both heartily, for papa and mama. You may wish Mr. and Mrs. Kincaid, and Jane, and Nilly, and Totty, and Baby, a very happy new year for us.

"Will you write a letter to papa on board ship, and finish it after you get to America, to send by the first ship? We all love you very much, and talk a great deal about you, and pray to God for you. Do you pray for us every day?

"My dear children, I must now bid you a most affectionate good bye.

"With much love, your Father."

One more letter from *the mother to her children*, must be placed on our pages; and it derives a mournful interest from its being *the last.* Before it reached the United States, she was resting in her grave, or rather, she was rejoicing in the presence of that Jesus to whom she had so lately sacrificed the society of her children:—

Ramree, Jan. 14, 1843.

"*To Lucy and Oliver.*

"MY DEAR, VERY DEAR CHILDREN,—

"I have written you many letters, considering that you are so *little children.* But I shall never tire in writing you, or thinking of you, or *loving* you. Though you are gone far, far away, where I shall never see you again in this world, yet you are still my own *dear, dear children,* and I never forget to pray many times every day that God will give you new, clean hearts; and that papa and mama may find their dear little lost ones in *heaven,* where we all may live for ever together, and love and praise the dear Saviour.

"My dear children, pray for yourselves every day. Love God; for he is good, very good to you; and you ought to love him with all your heart. *O how happy* will your papa and mama feel when we hear that Lucy and Olly are Christians, and have been baptized as Jesus was! Try to learn fast, and always obey grandpa, grandma, and Aunt L——. Love one another, and never speak an unkind word to each other. Do not go with children who do and say naughty things; and if any one says or does any thing that *you think* they ought not, tell Aunt L. all about it, and ask her if it is right. Aunt L. will be a mama to you, if you are good children. And God will be your Father, and will take care of you and bless you.

"Robert Stearns is well; he loves you both still, and sends a sweet kiss to each of you. Your baby-brother, Grover Samuel, grows fast, and is a good-natured laughing boy. We often say, 'How Lucy *would love* this little baby, if she were here; but you must think of him as your *dear brother*, and if God lets you both live, perhaps you may some time see him. Give grandpa, grandma, and Aunt L. a great deal of love from your mama and papa. Papa has been at Cheduba, and preached a long time to the people about Christ. They asked a great many questions about you, and seemed to love you. Pray for them. I send you each a book, which I promised you when I wrote it, with Ko En. Read it; and read your Burman Testament every day. I should be sorry to have you forget Burman. Talk together, occasionally, in Burman. If you do not like to talk before others, talk together by yourselves. But you need not feel ashamed to let others hear you. Write me a letter every month, when you have learned to write. Sometimes to papa and mama, and sometimes to Robert.

"Mr. De Silva goes to Kyouk Phyoo this evening, and will take this letter to a friend, who will send it to Calcutta to Mr. Roberts, and Uncle K.'s friend Captain Goodhue will, I think, take it to you across the great ocean.

"Now, with a great deal of love from papa and mama to Lucy and Olly, I am

"Your own Mama,

"SARAH D. C."

CHAPTER XI.

Increased devotion—Last letter to her Parents—The end of toil—Closing scenes in the life of Mrs. Comstock.

Toil on, courageous heart! toil on
  Till death shall give thee rest;
Thy labors here are not in vain,
  For heaven shall make them blest.
Thou shalt receive a rich reward,
  And shine, a brilliant gem,
When God shall make his jewels up,
  His precious diadem.

AFTER the departure of her dear children, Mrs. Comstock seemed to devote herself to the great work of evangelization with renewed ardor. God accepted her sacrifice, filled her mourning heart with heavenly peace, gave her greater desires to glorify him, and strength and grace to press on in the path of her pilgrimage. Never before was her interest in Missionary work more intense than now. Out of the very depths of her sorrow came forth a strong affection for those for whose sake she had borne it. Precious to her were the immortal interests of the heathen, more precious for those pangs of suffering.

"How great is the privilege," she exclaims, "of being permitted to do any thing for the salvation of souls from eternal death! To be instrumental in saving even *one soul!* O what a soul-inspiring idea! 'Tis worth the sacrifice, the cheerful, willing sacrifice of all that is dear, all that is prized of earthly blessing. If we may, at the 'great day,' behold *one soul* saved from endless woe, and raised to eternal joy and blessedness—if we may, with *one* soul saved through our instrumentality, join in the eternal song of praise around the throne, I shall feel that we are under an eternal debt of gratitude for the privilege of leaving all for a home in this land of darkness. When my heart is just ready to burst at the idea of never seeing my precious children more on earth, *that* thought buoys up my spirits, and enables me calmly and cheerfully to view the sacrifice. You will think I say a great deal on this subject; perhaps I do, more than is judicious, but you know I could never keep my thoughts and feelings from those I loved, and if you are ever a mother, and especially a mother among the heathen, far from every relative, where your children are your only companions, your only friends, you would cease to wonder at my feelings. Our children are *more* to *us* than children in America and other lands, are to *their* mothers. But the *greater* the sacrifice, the *dearer* will the cause for which it is made be to our hearts. I find it so in this case. I have never before felt so desirous to do *all* in my power to save souls; I have never felt so much tenderness of heart in telling the heathen of their Saviour; I have never, since I have been in this dark land, felt that brokenness of heart, that tenderness of spirit at a Throne of Grace, *as since I have given up my 'jewels' for Christ's sake.* If I am not deceived, I *do desire* to possess more of the Spirit of my Saviour, to live above the world, to be filled with the Spirit, that I may accomplish some little good while I sojourn here below."

We have already placed before our reader Mrs. Comstock's last letter to her children;

and in this place we will furnish an extract from her last communication to her beloved parents, under date of Jan. 11, 1843.

"Yesterday our hearts were cheered by the reception of letters from our loved native land. They were 'as cold water to a thirsty soul.' Sister Eunice Smith, of Rochester, gave us a detailed account of the glorious work of grace which has distinguished that city the last winter and spring. O! what a glorious season it must have been! I have felt my whole soul subdued while listening to the recital of what God has wrought. It seemed like bringing sacred things near. O! what a change would one such out-pouring of the Spirit effect in this idol-devoted province! The moral wilderness would truly become the garden of the Lord. And may we not hope to see such a day? Shall we not labor and pray for it? Yes; for 'nothing is too hard for the Lord.'

"My dear father and mother, do *you* love to plead before God the cause of poor, ruined Arracan? O, forget not the hundreds and thousands of her children, who, spell-bound, as it were, by the chains of idolatry and superstition, are rushing blindfold *down, down*, to the gulf of deep, dark despair. O, cease not, *frequently and fervently*, to bear them on your hearts to the feet of him who is 'mighty to save.' They are surely to be redeemed. Yes; I sometimes tell the natives, I *know* that this whole province *will* be converted from their foolish idols, and that they will yet acknowledge their Creator. Therefore, we faint not, though now they reject their only Saviour. God, who cannot lie, has promised it.

"Sometimes when I look forward, and contemplate that happy day, I feel, my dear parents, that it is a *great privilege* to be permitted to bear a humble part in preparing the way for its dawn, even though it be distant. I feel then that it was a privilege to give up all most dear on earth, for this object. Then my bereaved heart forgets its desolation, and I can think without a tear, yea, with calmness and cheerfulness, of the loved and lost, whom I am never more to behold in this wide world. But O, my mother, nothing else could tempt me to such a sacrifice; nothing else but *divine grace* could keep me from sinking under it. Sometimes still the thought that MY CHILDREN, yes, my *own* precious children, are forever riven from a mother's embrace,—that these eyes will never more behold,—that these lips will never more salute my own offspring, comes to my heart with such a withering, blighting influence, as almost to overwhelm me. Unaided, I could not sustain it. 'Is it possible?' I say to myself; and but for those two words of my Saviour, '*and children*,' in his enumeration of sacrifices for his sake, I should think it more than was required.

"But enough! Why do I always run on to this subject? It was certainly involuntary. But a mother's love knows how to throw a veil over her daughter's weakness. I will only add, *pray for them*, dear parents, pray in faith. They are the Lord's; consecrated to his service; and I wish all their education to be arranged and conducted in reference to *usefulness* in his cause. I believe he will convert them, and will accept the offering. It is the best I have to give, and I give them *cheerfully*."

Thus felt this bereaved mother, as she gathered to her breast the two little ones that remained, and girded herself anew for the work, committing those who had left her to the care of Him who "tempers the wind to the shorn lamb," and holds the waves in the hollow of his hand. Health and strength were given her, and a prospect of vigorous and uninterrupted labor for the good of the heathen.

But God had otherwise ordained. Her days were numbered, and were fast drawing toward their close. The end of her toil was nigh, though she perceived it not. Even before those darling children, whom she had sent to America, reached the home of their mother's childhood, she was no more.

By a sudden and mysterious providence, her life was closed at a time, when to short-sighted human vision, its prospect for usefulness was greatest. She was taken severely ill with dysentery, a disorder not uncommon among foreign residents in a tropical climate. The period of her sickness was short, and afforded but little opportunity for conversation, and the interchange of parting words.

Occasionally there were slight symptoms of amendment, but no permanent gain. Shortly before her death, she received a little nourishment from the hands of her husband, and remarked, that she felt relieved, and trusted soon to recover her lost strength. Mr. Comstock stepped out upon the verandah to inform the native Christians, anxiously waiting there, that there was still reason to hope. He heard her speak, and hastened back, just in time to see the shadow of death pass over her countenance, as she sank upon her pillow, and peacefully yielded up her spirit.

Thus, suddenly, on the 28th of April, 1843, after an illness of one week only, and at the early age of little more than thirty years, Mrs. Comstock passed away from the scenes of her early labors to her rest on high; leaving behind her, in that heathen land, two motherless babes, and many a mourner besides him who felt, in that trying hour, that death had bereaved him of his dearest treasure this side the grave.

It was a truly affecting scene which followed, as the tidings of her death were circulated. The natives sorrowed deeply over her unconscious clay, coming to the house by crowds in succession, to take a last look of their beloved friend and teacher.

This touching spectacle is thus described by Mr. Comstock in communicating to her friends in America this sad event. Says the bereaved husband:

"Her body was immediately surrounded by weeping and wailing heathen women, who felt that they had lost a friend. Such, indeed, was the case; for Mrs. C. truly loved and pitied the women of Arracan, and was never happier than when telling them of the Saviour. On the day after her death, as the news spread in the town, men, women, and children, (more of the last two,) began to crowd to my house; and it was estimated that about two thousand were here during the day. Their expressions of attachment to my dear wife, and of sorrow for her loss, were deeply affecting.

"'How kindly she always spoke to me, when she met me.'

"'She always gave us medicine, when we were sick.'

"'She was truly a good woman.' 'She

came here to die, far from her native land, with no mother or sister near her, because she pitied us.'

"Expressions similar to these were made and listened to, with many tears. I remarked once, 'what crowds are pressing to the house; are *all* from the town?' A by-stander replied, 'Yes, as the news spreads, all will be here, for she was greatly beloved.'

"Another added, 'Many tears will be shed in Ramree to-day.'"

Well might they weep; for it was for these,
Who whispered in tears her story;
She crossed the foam of the raging seas,
A herald of life and glory.

Well might they tell of the deeds she wrought
In her heavenly love and kindness;—
Of the lamp of eternal life she brought
To a world of sinful blindness.

For the voice that spake could speak no more,
In its tones of rapture swelling;—
And the wail that echoed from that wild shore,
Of the heathen's loss was telling.

She died,—but it was to live again in the precious fruits of heathen conversion, in the hearts of those who knew and loved her, in the brightest records of the Christian Church, and among the *faithful servants* who gather around the throne. Early her toils were closed: long ere the noon of her life was it, when they ceased; but before the hour came, the cause of Missions had received at her hands, and the hands of her husband, an impetus that shall be the means of opening a blissful eternity to thousands who sit in darkness, on whom are now dawning the rays of Divine truth, and who shall shine as stars in the crown of the sainted Missionary's rejoicing, forever and ever

Rest, loved one! rest, for thy work is done;
  Go, dust, to thy dreamless slumber;
Mount, soul, to the crown and the white robe won,
  And the bliss of the sainted number.

CHAPTER XII.

Brief review of her character—Noble faith—The fruit of toil—A husband's tribute—Death of her children in Arracan—The lonely laboror—Letter to his daughter—Last hours of Mr. Comstock—Plea for Arracan—Appeal to the Church.

"And I heard a voice from heaven, saying unto me, write, Blessed are the dead which die in the Lord from henceforth: Yea, saith the Spirit, that they may rest from their labors; and their works do follow them."

REVELATIONS XIV.

IN reviewing the character of so beloved and useful a woman, we scarcely know which most to admire, her whole-souled devotedness to the cause of Missions, her resolute, conscientious discharge of duty, her unwavering zeal, or that sublime faith, which, like the wings of an eagle, bore up her spirit aloft, over scenes of trial and suffering, enabling her to look beyond the present, to the end they were destined to accomplish. It was this same faith, also, that gave to her feeble woman's hand, strength and patience to sow the seed whose harvest should be for other eyes than hers;—while she was content to look down through the opening vista of the future, and behold it with a prophet's sight, as when she exclaims,

"I believe these hills and valleys of Arracan will yet leap at the sound of the church-going bell, and the hundreds and thousands of her children will be seen coming up from every city, village, and hamlet, with united heart and voice to the worship of the great Jehovah. It may not be in my day, but my children *may* see it. God grant that they may be privileged in hastening it on. *We* see but little fruit of our labor so far as *converts* are concerned, but we see the seed germinating. It is not dead; it will yet spring up; yea, this very seed we are now sowing, will spring up and yield a glorious harvest."

What a noble faith was this; a faith not to go unrewarded. Mrs. Comstock did not estimate the efficacy of the means she employed, by the visible results of her labors. She felt that it was for her to do her duty, and leave the result with Him in whose hands are all times, and ways, and seasons, for the accomplishment of His will. It would be impossible for one to live as she lived, among the heathen, toil as she toiled, and die as she died, without deeply affecting the mass of mind that surrounded her. The very fact of the weeping concourse who gathered around her remains, proves how *she* was regarded, who, for years, had been in and out among them, giving them the bread of life. Loving and esteeming her so much, could they but honor that religion of which her daily life had been so bright an embodiment. No, like leaven, silently but powerfully, her influence was at work among them, and will be until the end of time. Though while she lived, but a few turned from the homage of idols to the worship of the true God, many afterwards believed because of the words she spake, and many more will yet believe, the tidings of whose conversion may never reach our ears.

An affecting instance is related of one, who shortly after Mrs. Comstock's death, having been taught by her the way of salvation, gave evidence of a renewed heart. Mrs. C. had often conversed and prayed with her, and endeavored to lead her to the Saviour, but without any convincing result. She was much affected by the death of her beloved teacher, and manifested still deeper interest in religion. Shortly afterwards she was taken ill, and lay upon her death-bed. Her parents wished to invoke the aid of their gods in her behalf, and laid on her arms the charmed amulets, which should restore her. But she refused; her enlightened mind saw no power in these.

"Do not," she exclaimed, "practice any heathen rites on me; if I get well it will be by the power of God; if I die, it will be because it is His will, and I shall go and dwell with my teacher in heaven."

As death approached, she continued to profess strong faith in Christ, a willingness to die, and an assurance that her sins were forgiven, and she should be saved for the Saviour's sake. Thus she passed away, leaving behind her the joyful evidence, that her ransomed soul had gone to be reunited to her who had loved it so well.

We cannot close the narrative of this excellent woman and Christian better, than by giving the following tribute to her memory and worth, written by one who knew her best—her fellow-laborer and husband:

"The loss to the Mission by the death of Mrs. Comstock is very great. She eminently possessed many very desirable qualifications for a Missionary. Her kind spirit and affable manner secured for her the confidence and affection of all who knew her. She was endowed too with untiring patience and indomitable perseverance. I have often admired her patient and persevering efforts to impress religious truths upon the dark and vacant minds of a company of women from the country. The first remark from them, almost universally is, 'I don't understand.' She would then vary her language or subject, and keep varying it till they did understand, although to make them do so often seemed to me a hopeless task Her patience and perseverance, however, were not manifested to single companies alone. They were conspicuous through her whole course. Amid all her sicknesses and trials, which were many and great, she pursued the even tenor of her way; nothing daunted—endeavoring, as she had opportunity, to do good to all. She delighted in her work, and was never happier than when surrounded by women and children to whom she was telling the story of Christ crucified. She often, also, was compelled to engage in discussions with men, which she managed with great judgment.

"Although she was always desirous to go out with me to the villages, the circumstances of our family seldom permitted her to do so. However, whether left alone at home, or accompanying me in my tours, she always sought to be usefully employed, and her labors were abundant. She possessed a very good knowledge of the language, and her easy and correct use of it was often noticed by the natives with astonishment and admiration. Her industry and faithfulness, her love to souls and to Christ, her faith in God, and her mental and moral characteristics, as a whole, admirably fitted her for the station she occupied. Her health had been unusually good for a few months before her death, and her prospects of laboring long and successfully in Arracan were never fairer. But our thoughts were not God's thoughts. He had other designs, and called her to engage, I doubt not, in a higher sphere of enjoyment and usefulness. The Mission here is greatly weakened; but God hath done it, and all he does is right."

The young children of Mrs. Comstock did not long survive her to cheer the heart of the bereaved father in his lonely toil and grief.

Robert Stearns, the elder of the two, a boy of much promise, and of whom Mrs. C. had often written to her friends, in language of peculiar interest and affection, was the first to follow his mother to the spirit world. Then her darling babe drooped and died, and was laid by the side of its little brother.

Thus was affliction upon affliction appointed to the Missionary now left alone in that heathen world. Companions he still had in the work of his ministry, faithful and sympathising; but so far as near and dear human ties in that land were concerned, they had all been sundered, and he was emphatically alone.

But in those hours of anguish, there came to him help from One who is ever nigh to those who trust in Him, and whose hand is ever ready to wipe away their tears.

None but a child of God, who has experienced it, knows how great is the consoling power of religion in the severest sorrows of the soul. It sustained this mourning husband and father; God's grace was sufficient for him. He laid his beloved ones calmly in the grave, then putting his hand once more to the plough, looked not back, but pressed steadfastly on.

But we can gather his feelings best from his own language, with reference to this three-fold bereavement.

"I wrote you," he says, "just after the death of my dear Sarah, and, before this reaches you, I doubt not, you will have heard of the further chastening with which it has pleased our heavenly Father to visit me. June 12, at about two in the morning, my darling Robert breathed his last, after several hours of convulsive agony. He had been sick but three days. He was a remarkably intelligent and amiable boy, and was a great deal of society and comfort to me after his mother's death. July 1, my sweet babe left me, I doubt not, to join his mother and brother in heaven.

"How I felt as I watched the dying struggles of those dear ones, prepared their bodies for the grave, and conducted their burials, you cannot fully conceive, nor can you imagine the feeling which thoughts of them sometimes excite in my lonely heart.

"But my afflictions, although very severe and deeply felt, have been so tempered and controlled by the rich and abundant grace of the Lord Jesus, that I have been sustained and rendered peaceful, and at times, even joyful. *I had no adequate idea of the upholding and consoling power of faith in Christ, till earthly sources of happiness having entirely failed, I was left to look to Him alone for support and comfort.* He is, indeed, 'able to save unto the uttermost.' My earnest prayer is, that my chastening may yield the peaceable fruits of righteousness, and render me fully and permanently a partaker of God's holiness."

It will not it *cannot* be supposed that his

bereavements in Arracan would lessen Mr. Comstock's love to his children in America. The letter to his little daughter, which we now lay before the reader, shows his love to her, and his concern that she should never forget her mother, or her dear little brother.

Ramree, June 24, 1843.

"My dear Lucy,—

"Nine years ago to-day, your papa and mama were married in the Baptist meeting-house at Brookline. If you ask your Aunt L., she will tell you all about it. We lived very happily together eight years and ten months, and I always thank God for such a dear, good wife as your mama was; and I want you to thank him too, for such a mother. You know how she loved you, and always sought to make you happy and good. Her body lies now, on the small hill, with a little pagoda on the top of it, nearly in front of my house. It is the hill with some small idols on it, one of which, you or Olly, I have forgotten which, brought away, and when you put it back let it fall, and broke its head off. You will recollect the hill, I think.

"Your dear little brother, Robert, lies beside his mama; but I think both are holy, happy spirits in heaven. Robert was getting on in learning to read very well, and the day before he was taken sick, he learnt, among other words, 'father, mother, brother, sister,' which he repeated just before he died. He was a good boy, and a great deal of company and comfort to me, after your mama died. But God took him, and He does all things right.

"I have just been to talk and pray with Mah-sà-kéh, who is very sick, and will perhaps die. She sent for me to come and see her. She said that she was not afraid to die; she was a great sinner, but she believed in Christ, and prayed to him; and thought he would save her. When she heard that Robert was dead, she cried very much, and so did a good many other people, who knew him, and loved him. I have lately learnt, that Mah-sà-kéh begged her parents, with tears, to be baptized some time ago, saying she did not want to go to hell,—she wanted to be a Christian. You know how much your dear mama taught her, and prayed with her, and for her. I hope it was not in vain, and that she may be saved in consequence of it."

A few weeks after, giving her, in the same letter, an account of the death and funeral of the youngest child, he adds:—"There lie their bodies, but their pure and happy spirits dwell in the presence of God on high. Half the family are now, I trust, in heaven, and will you and Oliver immediately get ready to meet them there? Do not wait because you are young. Your brothers have died younger than you are, and you too may soon die. But should you live a great many years, there will be no better time for you to repent of sin and believe in Christ, than now. I am very anxious that you and Olly should become Christians immediately, and then, whether you live or die, all will be well.

"I feel very lonely, but the Lord is infinitely kind to me, and and often grants me his presence, which renders me calm and peaceful, amid all my sorrows. I am not very well, and am expecting to go to Sandoway in a day or two, to spend some time with Willard's papa and mama."

For a year after the death of his beloved wife and children, Mr. Comstock continued his faithful labors. At intervals he suffered from severe attacks of illness, when, to use his own language, he learned "to *suffer* as well as *labor* alone." But at length the message came for him also to leave the field and go home to his rest.

His last illness found him not unprepared. "I did desire," he said, "to live a little longer and labor for God; but if the Lord has no more for me to do, I can cheerfully leave the world now. I have no earthly cords to bind me here. My trust is in the Lord. He who has been with me thus far will still be with me, and take care of me. I have no fear to die; my faith is fixed on Jesus. I wish you to state distinctly to my friends at home, that I have *never in the least* regretted having come to this country."

He expired on the 25th of April, 1844, at the age of thirty-five years. He was a valuable man. Those who knew him best, considered him as admirably qualified to pioneer in the great work of evangelizing Arracan. During the last year of his life, he lamented much over the fewness of laborers in the Missionary field. The latest sentence he penned was upon this subject. It seemed at times almost to engross his thoughts. In his earnest plea to the Board, in behalf of Arracan, he says:—

"*American Baptists must give the gospel to this people or they perish forever.* Can you do nothing more for them?—*Can* not, and *will* not the many Baptist churches in America, which are feasting on spiritual blessings, spare the crumbs which fall from their tables for the famishing, dying thou sands of Arracan? Will they not, as a thank-offering, for their rich and numberless mercies, immediately send Missionaries to aid us in turning this people from their idols to the living God?"

The deep interest he felt in the redemption of Arracan had manifested itself most vividly, on the occasion of the departure of his children to America. Amidst the anguish of that hour, which only a parent can conceive, there was room still in his burdened heart for the welfare of Zion; his last words were a plea in her behalf.

The Rev. Mr. Kincaid says, "Never shall I forget the words, or the tone in which those words were uttered, as he turned up his face, still bedewed with tears, and exclaimed, as the boat moved away,

"'*Remember, Brother Kincaid, six men for Arracan?*'"

Men were sent at last, but not until God had removed yet another from the few laborers already there, and the faithful Missionary slept with his beloved babes and the partner of his toils nnder the turf of that land for whose evangelization he had labored and plead.

Thus one after another of the toil-worn servants of the cross fall upon the field of labor. One after another enter into the glorious rest that remaineth to the people of God, and the wailing nations desire the coming of others, who shall carry on the blest work of publishing the glad tidings of eternal life. Who will follow in the paths of the noble pioneers for a lost world's redemption? Who will supply the places made vacant by death?

Not from the votaries of pleasure, the lovers of this world, and the worshipers at its shrines, may we look for aid, but from among those who are heirs of a heavenly inheritance, and who have enlisted under the banner of the cross. Men who are willing to *toil* for Christ's sake, in obedience to the command, "Go teach all nations."

We know that God, if he choose, can convert nations in a day, that he can accomplish, in a few short weeks, a work for which his people might labor for years; but the fact of such Divine power does not exempt us from unceasing efforts. We are commanded to do our duty, to sow in faith the seed, and await the time of God. In this respect, especially, the example of the beloved subject of this memoir is worthy of serious consideration. Like her let us go forward, and do with our might, whatsoever our hand findeth to do.

Above all, let us possess and cultivate genuine faith. Month after month, year after year we assemble and pray, that God would bless the labors of his servants in foreign fields, and turn many to righteousness, but when the signs of the times are, that God is about to do this, as already among the millions of China, what a thrill of astonishment and fear runs through the Christian church! Had we prayed in faith, looking for the blessing, would this be? Are we prepared by expectation for the signal manifestations of God? for the glorious dawn of the Sun of Righteousness, with whose beams of mercy the Orient is already tinged?

O! let us awake from our sleep; the night is far spent; the morning is at hand! Let us speed on the great work of salvation, and cheer the fainting hearts of those who labor afar off. Let the crumbs from our tables be no longer the famishing heathen's portion, but the bread of life in its rich abundance, that they may partake and live forever.

Church of the Living God! arise
  And do thy Master's holy will,
Plead for his grace with tears and sighs,
  Till every promise he fulfill.

THE END.

www.ingramcontent.com/pod-product-compliance
Lightning Source LLC
La Vergne TN
LVHW050530100826
845148LV00002B/502

* 9 7 8 1 4 2 5 5 1 9 4 4 5 *